THE GODWINS

THE RISE AND FALL OF
A NOBLE DYNASTY

The family of Earl Godwin of Wessex stands among the most famous in English history. Owing their rise to Godwin's outstandingly successful career during the reign of the Danish King Cnut (1016–35), they became even more prominent in the time of Edward the Confessor (1042–66). Godwin's daughter, Edith, became King Edward's wife, his son Harold inherited his father's earldom of Wessex, his son Tostig acquired Northumbria and other sons also became earls. Over the century they accumulated great wealth and established enormous influence.

However, Edith and Edward could not have children and ultimately this destabilised the monarchy, exposing the problem of the royal succession after Edward's death. Harold took the throne soon after but was defeated and killed at the Battle of Hastings in 1066; Queen Edith lived in England until her death in 1075, and other survivors of Godwin's family faded into obscurity.

Frank Barlow places the Godwins at the centre of this unstable world, charting the family through to Harold – the last Anglo-Saxon king – and finally the crowning of William the Conqueror during the Norman Conquest.

Frank Barlow is the author of many books including the bestselling 'The Feudal Kingdom of England'. He is Emeritus Professor of History at the University of Exeter and Honorary Fellow of St John's College, Oxford; CBE, FBA, FRSL.

THE GODWINS

THE RISE AND FALL OF
A NOBLE DYNASTY

FRANK BARLOW

London • New York • Toronto • Sydney • Tokyo • Singapore
Hong Kong • Cape Town • Madrid • Paris • Amsterdam • Munich • Milan

PEARSON EDUCATION LIMITED

Head Office:
Edinburgh Gate
Harlow CM20 2JE
Tel: +44 (0)1279 623623
Fax: +44 (0)1279 431059
www.pearsoned.co.uk

First published in Great Britain in 2002

© Pearson Education Limited 2002, 2003

The right of Frank Barlow to be identified as Author
of this Work has been asserted by him in accordance
with the Copyright, Designs and Patents Act 1988.

ISBN 0 582 78440 9

British Library Cataloguing in Publication Data
A CIP catalogue record for this book can be obtained from the British Library

Library of Congress Cataloging in Publication Data
A CIP catalog record for this book can be obtained from the Library of
Congress

10 9 8 7 6 5 4 3 2 1

Typeset in 10.5/13pt Galliard by Graphicraft Limited, Hong Kong
Printed and bound in China
EPC/01

The Publishers' policy is to use paper manufactured from sustainable forests.

CONTENTS

CONTENTS

GENERAL EDITOR'S PREFACE

The family of Earl Godwin of Wessex must be among the most famous in English history. Owing their rise to Godwin's outstandingly successful career during the reign of the Danish King Cnut (1016–35), they became even more prominent in the time of Edward the Confessor (1042–66). Godwin's daughter Edith became the king's wife, his son Harold inherited his father's earldom of Wessex, another son Tostig acquired Northumbria, arguably the next most important earldom in the kingdom after Wessex, and other sons also became earls. In 1065, under Edith's patronage, an anonymous Flemish monk began the so-called *Vita Ædwardi Regis,* a text intended to be a tribute to the family's greatness. Yet within little more than a year, all was in ruins. The childlessness of Edith's and Edward's marriage always threatened to open up the problem of the royal succession after Edward's death. Harold and Tostig quarrelled. Although Harold took the throne after Edward's death and defeated an invasion led by the King of Norway and his brother Tostig, he was himself defeated and killed at the Battle of Hastings. On 25 December 1066 William the Conqueror was crowned king of the English in Westminster Abbey. Queen Edith lived on in England until her death in 1075. Other survivors of Godwin's family faded into obscurity. Even the location of Harold's physical remains became the subject of uncertainty. The most tangible, if frequently inscrutable, direct record of the family's rise and fall is the truncated text of the *Vita Ædwardi*, its author grappling painfully with the disasters which had engulfed his subjects while he was writing.

As Frank Barlow points out in an introductory historio-graphical survey, it has always been well nigh impossible to detach the history of the Godwin family from the history of the Norman Conquest. This is partly because some of the main sources on which we have to rely were written to praise William of Normandy, and so vilified his rival. It is also true that modern historians' perceptions of the Conquest have frequently influenced the way they view Godwin and his offspring. It is Professor Barlow's achievement in his deservedly famous *Edward the Confessor* and in the present book to set out to assess his subjects' actions freed from hindsight, without any connection to an event which they could not possibly have foreseen. As the modern editor of the *Vita Ædwardi*, Frank Barlow tells their remarkable story from the basis of a long and unique acquaintance with this allusive and difficult source. The complexities of politics are as a result explored with remarkable subtlety and sensitivity, and the undoubted simplifications of the Norman sources are rejected. Godwin is presented as a crafty survivor, Harold as the more able of the two brothers and Edith as an educated, capable, but sometimes unsympathetic personality. The ambivalence which Edward must often have felt towards his wife's seemingly all-pervasive family is made manifest. The context of an English kingdom linked by long history and dynastic claims to Scandinavia and the troubled politics of a kingdom disrupted by regular succession crises is clearly set out. There are intriguing commentaries on the family's treatment in modern fiction and on the fate of their descendants. And Professor Barlow's recent new edition of another crucial source, the *Carmen de Hastingae Proelio*, is used to provide an original and challenging account of the Battle of Hastings.

Frank Barlow's *The Godwins* is an exceptionally welcome addition to the Medieval World series. As the editor of some of the central sources for his subject, the author of many books and articles on the eleventh and twelfth centuries, and in particular of three outstanding medieval biographies of Edward the Confessor, William Rufus and Thomas Becket, he is superbly qualified to write the authoritative history of a great noble family and to assess the wider significance of their role in English history. Here he reminds us that Harold is often thought of as an English national hero. Yet while the family's fall is unquestionably seen as possessing elements of tragedy, *The Godwins* provides a masterly display of how to unravel sources written in a very different thought-world from our own and of the complexities of the world of eleventh-century politics.

David Bates

PREFACE TO THE PAPERBACK EDITION

For this edition I have corrected one error and made a number of small revisions. A good number of these are due to correspondents who have kindly provided me with information or offered opinions. I wish to thank especially Miss Dinah Dean of Waltham Abbey, the author of a novel about Harold's daughter, Gytha, called *Daughter of the Sunset Isles*, and Mrs Patricia A. Millward of Heddon on the Wall. The Editor-in-Chief, Heather McCallum, and the Development Editor, Magda Robson, continue to guide my steps.

F.B.

AUTHOR'S PREFACE

When I was an undergraduate, my tutor, Austin Lane Poole, once accused me of laziness. This was, I think, a little unfair, as, after four years spent in the excellent History sixth form at Newcastle High School under the admirable Mr Lush, I was finding it easy to relax and enjoy all the pleasures that Oxford had to offer. Poole had the excuse that a whole line of history scholars at St John's had recently gone astray — one had even become a disciple of the Satanist, Aleister Crowley. But the charge rankled, and I have spent many years proving him wrong. It was, therefore, with great pleasure that I received the invitation from my former pupil at Exeter, David Bates, to contribute a book on the Godwins to his Medieval World series, for this would not only round off my studies of England in the eleventh century but also keep me occupied in my old age. It also means that I have almost turned full circle, for after dallying for some years in the twelfth and thirteenth centuries, it was in 1962 that my edition of *The Life of King Edward who rests at Westminster* made its first appearance and my *William I* was commissioned by A.L. Rowse for his Teach Yourself History series.

In writing this book I have profited from a good number of publications, both old and new, devoted to some aspects of the Norman Conquest; and I hope I have acknowledged my indebtedness in the notes. I have had an interesting correspondence with Rhona Beare, with a gift of some of her articles, on the enigmatic poem in *Vita*. I am indebted to Hubert J. Grills for a photocopy of the article by Lundie W. Barlow, which otherwise I would have missed. I have been encouraged and helped by Professor Bates and aided by all the editorial team. Alison Bowers copy-edited my text and very kindly contributed the Bibliography. The Editor-in-Chief, Heather McCallum, and Magda Robson guided my steps to publication. To all those who have helped me, my grateful thanks.

F.B.

LIST OF GENEALOGIES

LIST OF PLATES

The plates can be found in the centre of the book.

ABBREVIATIONS

ANS	*Proceedings of the Battle Conference on Anglo-Norman Studies*, vols 1–11 (1979–89), ed. R. Allen Brown, vols 12–16 (1990–5), ed. M. Chibnall, vols 17–24 (1996–2002), ed. C. Harper-Bill.
ASC	*The Anglo-Saxon Chronicle: A collaborative edition in 23 volumes* (Cambridge, 1996–). Trans. D. Whitelock, in *EHD*, i. 109–110, 135–235; printed separately as *The Anglo-Saxon Chronicle*, ed. D. Whitelock with D.C. Douglas and S.I. Tucker (1961).
Barlow, *EC*	F. Barlow, *The English Church, 1000–1066* (London, 2nd edn, 1979); *The English Church, 1066–1154* (London, 1979).
Barlow, *Edward*	*Edward the Confessor*, Yale English Monarchs (New Haven and London, 1997).
Barlow, *William Rufus*	*William Rufus*, Yale English Monarchs (New Haven and London, 2000).
Brevis Relatio	*Brevis Relatio de Guillelmo nobilissimo comite Normannorum*, ed. E.M.C. van Houts, Camden Miscellany, xxxiv, Camden 5th ser., x (1997), 1–48.

BT	*The Bayeux Tapestry*, ed. F.M. Stenton (London, 2nd edn, 1965).
Carmen	*The* Carmen de Hastingae Proelio *of Guy bishop of Amiens*, ed. and trans. F. Barlow (OMT, 1999).
DB	*Domesday Book.*
EC	see Barlow, *EC*.
EHD	*English Historical Documents*, i (*c*. 510–1042), ed. D. Whitelock (London, 1968); ii (1042–1189), ed. D.C. Douglas and G.W. Greenaway (2nd edn, 1981).
Encomiast, the	The author of *Vita*.
Encomium Emmae	*Encomium Emmae Reginae*, ed. A. Campbell (Royal Hist. Soc., Camden 3rd ser., lxxii, 1949).
FNC	E.A. Freeman, *The History of the Norman Conquest of England* (i, ii, 2nd edn, 1870; iii–v, 1st edn, 1869–75).
Freeman, *NC*	See *FNC*.
Gaimar	*Lestoire des Engleis par Geffrei Gaimar*, ed. A. Bell, 3 vols (Anglo-Norman Texts Soc. xiv–xvi, Oxford, 1960).
GG	*The Gesta Guillelmi of William of Poitiers*, ed. and trans. R.H.C. Davis and M. Chibnall (OMT, 1998).
GND	*The* Gesta Normannorum Ducum *of William of Jumièges, Orderic Vitalis, and Robert of Torigni*, ed. E.M.C. van Houts, 2 vols (OMT, 1992–5).
GR	William of Malmesbury, *De Gestis regum Anglorum*, ed. N.E.S.A. Hamilton (Rolls ser., 1870) (used here); ed. and trans. R.A.B. Mynors,

	R.M. Thomson and M. Winterbottom (OMT, 1998).
John of Worcester	*The Chronicle of John of Worcester*, ii, ed. R.R. Darlington and P. McGurk, trans. J. Bray and P. McGurk (OMT, 1995).
K/Kemble/*KCD*	J.M. Kemble, *Codex diplomaticus aevi Saxonici* (London, 1839–48).
Keynes	S. Keynes, *The Diplomas of King Æthelred 'the Unready', 978–1016* (Cambridge, 1980).
King Harald's Saga	In Book III of Snorri Sturluson's *Heimskringla*, trans., with introduction, by M. Magnusson and N. Pálsson (Penguin, London, 1966).
Körner	S. Körner, *The Battle of Hastings: England and Europe 1035–1066* (Lund, 1964).
Lloyd	J.E. Lloyd, *A History of Wales from the Earliest Times to the Edwardian Conquest*, ii (London, 3rd edn, 1939).
OMT	Oxford Medieval Texts.
OV	Orderic Vitalis, *Historia Ecclesiastica*, ed. M. Chibnall, 6 vols (OMT, 1969–80).
Rolls ser.	Chronicles and Memorials of Great Britain and Ireland during the Middle Ages, published under the direction of the Master of the Rolls (London, 1858–96).
Sawyer/S.	P.H. Sawyer, *Anglo-Saxon Charters: an Annotated List and Bibliography* (R. Hist. Soc., 1968).
Stafford	P. Stafford, *Queen Emma and Queen Edith* (1997). Blackwell, Oxford.

Vita	*The Life of King Edward who rests at Westminster*, ed. and trans. F. Barlow, 2nd edn (OMT, 1992).
Vita Haroldi	Ed. W. de Gray Birch (1885), trans. M. Swanton, *Three Lives of the Last Englishmen* (1984), 3–41.
Vita Wulfstani	*The Vita Wulfstani of William of Malmesbury*, ed. R.R. Darlington, Royal Hist. Soc., Camden 3rd ser., xl (1928).
Walker	I.W. Walker, *Harold, The last Anglo-Saxon King* (Stroud: Sutton, 1997).

INTRODUCTION

The Godwins were one of the grandest noble families in England in the first half of the eleventh century. The eponym married the sister-in-law of King Cnut; his daughter Edith married King Edward the Confessor; five of his sons became earls, and one of them, Harold, succeeded Edward on the English throne. The family came to possess vast estates almost throughout the English shires. It was, however, a meteoric rise — and fall. Not only is Godwin's ancestry uncertain, but also the whole dynasty crashed to ruin in the battles of 1066, merely thirteen years after his death and fifty years after the beginning of his climb to power.

It was a period of violent upheavals in English history.[1] Viking attacks in the ninth century, which had threatened to take the kingdom within a Scandinavian orbit, if not empire, were checked by Alfred the Great (king, 871–899). But after the 'imperial' triumphs in Britain of Alfred's grandson, King Æthelstan (924–939), and the peaceful reign of Alfred's great-grandson, Edgar (957–975), the rule of Edgar's son, Æthelred 'the Unready' (978–1013, 1014–1016), was a disaster. It saw the resumption of viking raids which culminated in the conquest of England by Danish kings, first Swegen Forkbeard (1013–1014) and then his son Cnut (1016–1035). Cnut, after initial barbarities, reestablished orderly and consensual government; but his dynasty was not long extended by his two sons who ruled in turn, Harold Harefoot (1035–1040) and Harthacnut (1040–1042); and it was left to Æthelred's son, Edward the Confessor (1042–1066), Anglo-Norman by blood, to reconfirm the Old-English monarchy. But Edward's child-lessness in the end again destabilized the monarchy and led to the Norman conquest.

The chequered history of the monarchy between 1016 and 1066 contributed to a similar instability in the aristocracy. Dynasties rose and fell. For example, a Mercian family headed in Æthelred's reign by Eadric Streona was destroyed by Cnut. But by and large until 1066 there was considerable biological continuity among the the nobles (thegns) and their élite, the ealdormen, the provincial governors. Among these, the Godwins were the most successful and the best publicized by the chroniclers. The Norman conquest, however, unlike the Danish conquest, did not modify, but virtually destroyed the existing Anglo–Danish nobility. Although today it is not unusual for an English family to claim, usually fancifully, that its ancestor came over with William the Conqueror, few even attempt to push their pedigree further back into Old-English society.[2]

To appreciate the status and careers of the Godwins it is helpful to have an understanding of the social set-up in the kingdom of England in their time. This political entity had evolved out of the Germanic conquests and settlements in Roman Britain in the fifth and sixth centuries AD. In the beginning there had been a multiplicity of petty kings and kingdoms; but between the sixth and the tenth centuries, through amalgamations and the extinction of royal dynasties, the kingdoms had been reduced to three, Wessex, Mercia and Northumbria; and in 927 Æthelstan, king of the West Saxons and Mercians, annexed Northumbria. However, memory of the ancient kingdoms, several perpetuated as shires, persisted; and in times of stress, such as the viking eras, the united kingdom could easily break up again on ancient fault lines. Nevertheless, there was a strong consciousness of an English people in an English kingdom. As early as 731 the Venerable Bede had written his famous *Ecclesiastical History of the English Nation* (*Anglorum gens*). And ruling the kingdom of the English were English kings — whatever their racial origins may have been.

The victorious royal dynasty, that of the West Saxons, traced back to Cerdic (a Celtic name), who died in 534; and Cerdic was described as the ninth generation from Woden, the Germanic god of war, after whom the fourth day of the week, Wednesday, is called. Woden signifies 'the furious' or 'the madman', and was rather strangely identified by the Romans with their god, Mercury. Succession to the West-Saxon kingship, although hereditary, was not according to the rules of primogeniture; and, if the obvious successor did not emerge, there could be conflict or a division of the lands between rival claimants. Occasionally a candidate appeared unexpectedly from a collateral branch of the family and fought his way to the throne. In the period 1013–1066, owing to the Danish conquests and Edward the Confessor's childlessness, succession to the English throne was exceptionally disturbed and unsettling.

The king ruled over subjects who, according to the law codes and treatises, were strictly stratified. In the eleventh century the main strata were ealdormen (earls), thegns and ceorls (churls); and each had rights and duties defined by the law. Beneath these was a large layer of slaves, who had no legal rights. Earls and thegns formed the nobility, and the ceorls were the ordinary freemen. The ealdorman was the royal officer in charge of a territory, usually one of the old kingdoms or sometimes one or more shires. In the post-Danish period, through the influence of the corresponding Scandinavian title *jarl*, the vernacular word became *eorl* (earl). In the witness lists in royal charters written in Latin, he is *dux*, which can be translated as 'duke'; but after the Norman Conquest he was reduced to *comes* (count). The thegns formed the mass of the nobility. The literal sense of the word is 'mature' or 'strong'; but in the witness lists the thegn is styled *minister*, which means a servant, particularly an armed retainer, a warrior; and this links his rank with his relationship to his master, the king. There were also thegns in the service of earls and even of other thegns. After the Norman Conquest the Latin equivalent was *miles*, a knight. The value of a ceorl's life (his *wergild*) in Mercia was 200 shillings, that of a thegn six times as much (1200 shillings); and an earl's may have been thirty times as much (6000 shillings).[3] The value of their oaths in a court of law was in the same proportions. It would seem that in the eleventh century the English aristocracy obtained greater revenues from their estates and displayed their new wealth conspicuously. This was to be seen not only in their clothes and food but also in new buildings, including churches.[4]

None of these hereditary social classes was homogeneous or completely exclusive. According to a treatise on status written at the beginning of the eleventh century,[5] ceorls and merchants could so prosper as to become entitled to the rights of a thegn. The qualification needed by a ceorl was the full possession of five hides of land, a church and kitchen, a bell-house and a fortified gate-house, and a special office in the king's hall. A trader qualified by three crossings of the open sea at his own expense. Similarly, a thegn, if appointed to an earldom by the king, enjoyed an earl's rights. Hence, although society was divided into hereditary castes, with the law defining the value of their lives and oaths and most other rights and duties, a limited amount of mobility was envisaged and must have occurred. The legend that Earl Godwin was the son of a Sussex churl, and that the family progressed from churl to king in three generations, wonderfully exemplifies these aspirations.

In a tripartite division of society the king and the nobility were the *bellatores*, the warriors, as distinct from the *oratores*, the priests, and the *laboratores*, the manual workers. And the king and his earls were expected to lead the armed forces against the enemy. In the war against vikings the English army was called by the annalists a *fyrd*, the Danish a *here*. Both words are unspecific and cover anything from a small raiding party to an army to be counted in thousands. The nucleus of any English army commanded by a king or an earl were the 'hearth-troops', the housecarls, the armed retainers who were in constant attendance on their lord and were maintained by him in his household. These bodyguards seem in this period to have been mostly vikings. Beyond these were the commander's thegns, and there were also the soldiers owed by the localities according to their rateable value, often one man from every five hides or six carucates of land. For local defence any able-bodied man might lend a hand.

All the soldiers were horsemen, and their equipment is shown — perhaps ideally — on the Bayeux Tapestry, made in the 1070s. They wore in battle a coat of chain mail, the byrnie, which reached to the knees, a conical helmet with a nasal, and puttees on the legs. Their weapons were the long sword and the two-handed battle axe. Archers are rarely mentioned in accounts of English armies of the period; but the bow must have been used in hunting; and one English archer is shown on the tapestry[6] (in contrast to the many Norman archers). On this evidence bowmen were not a regular constituent element of an English or Danish army. All these troops normally rode to battle, but fought on foot. They attacked in column or in line according to the terrain or the commander's tactical choice. But the preferred English tactic was to stand as a massed phalanx in defence, if possible based on a suitable site, a hill or a position reinforced by ditches or walls. Because of the reluctance to attack unless enjoying an obvious superiority in numbers, pitched battles were rare. But in all encounters men fought hand to hand with bloody results. A commander's men were supposed to fight to their death with their lord — and sometimes did. There were no chivalric conventions: prisoners seem seldom to have been taken and there is no talk of ransoms. To the victors the spoils! The corpses were stripped and left to those other scavengers of the field, the birds, the wolves and the dogs. The qualities prized in kings and nobles were, there-fore, leadership, physical strength, courage and loyalty, although craftiness was not despised.

With England part of an island and subject to viking raids, a navy was essential and was raised in several ways. Some coastal areas were responsible for the provision of ships: groups of three hundreds had to produce a longship with sixty oarsmen, that is to say, as with the army, one man for every five hides of land. Ships could be requisitioned from the sea ports, and Edward the Confessor made a special arrangement in 1051 with the 'Cinque Ports', Dover, Sandwich, Romney, Hythe and Fordwich, for the supply of vessels. And mercenary viking units could be hired. From 1012 until 1051, when Edward paid off the last five ships, the English kings had such foreign crews in service. At times of danger, certainly in the early years of Edward's reign, the fleet was mobilized once a year in early summer at Sandwich in Kent. And with the fleet were the king and many of his leading nobles. Godwin and his sons, with their earldoms' contingents, seem always to have been there. As no naval battles occurred, the purpose would seem to have been both preventive and intimidatory; and the ships could also be used to transport troops from place to place.

Godwin himself had no reputation as an outstanding sol-dier,[7] and he seems, for lack of opportunity after 1017, to have been seldom on campaign and never in battle. But his five eldest sons all had military experience, and four of them per-ished in battle in 1066. Godwin and Gytha bred a family of warriors of whom the family's encomiast was proud.

Anglo-Saxon personal names have always caused difficulties. Indeed, they have been considered by many observers, includ-ing the Norman conquerors, as uncouth and barbarous.[8] Men and women of the free classes normally were given a two-part baptismal name; and the men sometimes also acquired a sur-name, occasionally an epithet or nickname (by-name), but often identifying their father (a patronymic). The first names were permuted within the family. Among the nobility common prefixes were Ethel- or Elf-, meaning 'noble' and Ead- or Ed-, meaning 'happy' or 'blessed'. For example, the sons of King Edward the Elder, King Alfred's son, were named Elf-weard, Ethel-stan, Ed-win, Ed-mund and Ead-red, while his daughters were called Elf-gifu, Ethel-hild, Ead-burgh, Ead-flaed, Ead-gyth and Ead-hild. Not only have many of these names gone completely out of use, but also how they should be spelled in modern histories is contentious. The great Victorian medieval historian, E.A. Freeman, strove to reintroduce and popularize the original and 'authentic' forms. In his works King Alfred is 'Ælfred', King Edgar 'Eadgar', King Edward 'Eadweard', and the several ladies Edith are 'Eadgyth'. For him it was a matter of principle and he quarrelled bitterly with the editor of the *Dictionary of National Biography* over it. The usual practice today, with and following F.M. Stenton, is to give the name in its modern form when one is available and especially when the historical character is well known under it, for example Alfred, Edgar, Edward and Edith. A few names, however, such as Tosti/Tostig still divide opinion. In the following pages pedantry has, when possible, been avoided.

Notes

1. F.M. Stenton's *Anglo-Saxon England*, first published in 1943, remains the best survey of the period. But see also P.H. Blair, *Anglo-Saxon England* (1959), H.R. Loyn, *Anglo-Saxon England and the Norman Conquest* (1962), P.H. Sawyer, *From Roman Britain to Norman England* (1978), and Ian Howard, *Swein Forkbeard's Invasions and the Danish Conquest of England, 991–1017* (2003). A useful guide to recent scholarship in the field is *A Companion to the Anglo-Norman World*, ed. Christopher Harper-Bill and Elisabeth van Houts (2003).
2. Cf. J.H. Round, *Family Origins and other Studies*, ed. William Page (1930), which contains a full bibliography of his genealogical publications.

3. *EHD*, i. 433.
4. R. Fleming, 'The new wealth, the new rich and the new political style in late Anglo-Saxon England', *ANS*, xxiii (2000), 1–22.
5. *EHD*, i. 432.
6. *BT*, pl. 63.
7. The encomiast, since he always stresses the earl's patience and love of peace, pays him on this subject what could be considered the minimum compliments possible: *Vita*, 10–11 and 40–1.
8. *GR*, i. 44–5, 120.

SOURCES

The sources for the history of the Godwin family are largely the same as for the English kingdom and monarchy.[1] They are discussed in several of the modern histories of this period, notably in E.A. Freeman's *History of the Norman Conquest of England* and F.M. Stenton's *Anglo-Saxon England*. See also Frank Barlow, *Edward the Confessor*. Of special value is Sten Körner's *The Battle of Hastings: England and Europe* (1964), in which he takes a critical and rather sceptical look both at the primary sources and also at their treatment by modern historians.

The primary authority is *The Anglo-Saxon Chronicle*, written in the vernacular, which survives in three main versions for the eleventh century, 'C', 'D' and 'E'.[2] As these are derived from 'X', a lost common ancestor, when in agreement they do not corroborate. Each is slanted. For Edward the Confessor's reign, the 'C' version, made at Abingdon Abbey in Berkshire, is royalist in tone, whereas the 'E' version, written at St Augustine's Abbey at Canterbury, is usually Godwinist. The chronicle is also a source for most twelfth-century English chronicles written in Latin, such as those of John of Worcester, William of Malmesbury, Henry of Huntingdon and Symeon of Durham.

Completely independent of the English tradition is the Norman version of events, a quite different story, in which Godwin and his son Harold are the villains. The basic text could have been a justification for the conquest of England prepared by William's advisers in 1066 for circulation among the rulers of Europe and directed particularly at the pope. Cardinal Hildebrand, the future Pope Gregory VII, certainly became an advocate of William's claim and secured the mission of a papal banner and perhaps some other spiritual aids. The propaganda campaign led to the penitential for William's army issued about 1070 by the papal agent, Ermenfrid Bishop of Sion in Switzerland, in which the penances for the different classes of soldier are laid down. This cleansing of the Norman army after the reformation of the English church also marks the start of the literary commemoration and apologia. Beginning with William of Jumièges's section in the *Gesta Normannorum Ducum*, written about 1070–1,[3] it is developed in the so-called History, written by William of Poitiers, Archdeacon of Lisieux, before about 1077.[4] For his account of William's invasion of England in 1066 the archdeacon also used a poem (*Carmen*) on the event, now securely identified as the work of the non-Norman, Guy Bishop of Amiens, produced almost immediately after the battle of Hastings, probably in 1067.[5] The stream of historical writing reached its flood with Orderic Vitalis's *Ecclesiastical History*, a large work in thirteen books.[6] A half-English monk in a Norman abbey, writing in the first decades of the twelfth century, he tried to harmonize both traditions.

Meanwhile the Bayeux Tapestry had been produced, probably both designed and manufactured in the 1070s at St Augustine's Abbey, Canterbury, and presumably for the earl of Kent, Odo Bishop of Bayeux, the Conqueror's half-brother.[7] It illustrates in strip-cartoon fashion Anglo-Norman relations from 1064 or 1065 until October 1066. Its ending is now lost, but it probably finished with William's coronation at Westminster on Christmas Day. Its story is based mainly on the Norman sources, primarily William of Poitiers's *Gesta Guillelmi*. But the designer seems to have known *Vita Ædwardi Regis* and his treatment of the events is notably dispassionate. It is an interpretation of the Norman conquest in terms of the secular epics of France, the *chansons de geste*.[8] Harold is the noble warrior who betrays his feudal lord by breaking the oath he had taken him on the relics of the church of Bayeux, and is punished for his disloyalty. In the borders are scenes from Aesop's fables concerned with treachery. For us, the tapestry's main interest lies in its illustration of the events, although, as many of the scenes are modelled on pre-existing Canterbury manuscript designs, they cannot be considered completely trustworthy representations, especially when depicting Normans.

Scandinavian sources contribute little to mainstream English history and less to the story of the Godwins, partly because of lack of interest, partly because of their relative lateness. But the histories by the German, Adam of Bremen, the Dane, Saxo Grammaticus, and the Icelander Snorri Sturluson (murdered in 1241), provide a little, sometimes untrustworthy, detail.[9]

Unusually, there are also two Latin literary works, each commissioned by an English queen and both apparently designed to influence the succession to the throne. The earlier, the so-called *Encomium Emmae Reginae*, was entrusted by Emma, widow in turn of Kings Æthelred and Cnut, to an inmate of one of the convents at Saint-Omer in Flanders, maybe St Bertin's, during the short reign of her son, Harthacnut (1040–1042).[10] Written entirely from a Danish standpoint, but in no way hostile to the English, it gives a view, presumably largely Emma's, of Danish–English history from 1013, and stresses that throne-worthiness, at least after 1017 when she married Cnut, was derived solely through her. The tract is, therefore, composed in favour of Harthacnut, their only son, against all others, particularly Cnut's children from other women. But it must have been directed more immediately against her one surviving son from her first marriage to King Æthelred, Edward, later known as 'the Confessor', who had returned to England in 1041. Since, however, the Encomiast regarded Edward and Harthacnut as full brothers (he never mentions Æthelred), he may have allowed Edward residual rights to the throne. Edward's younger brother, Alfred, had been killed in England when he returned from Normandy in 1037. Earl Godwin, as well as King Harold Harefoot, had been involved in his murder; but the Encomiast treats the earl circumspectly. Perhaps he could see a little farther into the future than his patron.

The later tract is the so-called *Vita Ædwardi Regis*, commissioned by Queen Edith, Godwin's daughter, from a foreign clerk, again it would seem from Saint-Omer, probably shortly before Edward's death. It is a eulogy of her family, obviously intended to prepare for its taking over the government in some way after Edward's death.[11] This tells the story of the Godwins from Edith's point of view. But because events moved so quickly and unexpectedly in 1066, the author of *Vita* seems to have lost his way. And the tract, when cleansed of its Godwinist elements, became the ur-text in Edward the Confessor's hagiography. Although its evidence has to be used with caution, it provides a livelier, more intimate view of the actors than can be found elsewhere.

Unfortunately, the only surviving manuscript is defective. It has lost, it would seem, the centre leaves of the first and last gatherings, eight pages in all, causing two lacunae each of some 1,200 words. The second was concerned not with the Godwins but with Edward's post-mortem miracles. The first, however, dealt with Godwin's children. The gap in this chapter (2) can be reconstructed only in part from derivative writers. William of Malmesbury and Osbert of Clare both borrowed a sentence or two about Edith's marriage to King Edward and her eminent suitability for queenship. But the fourteenth-century Westminster monk, Richard of Cirencester, in the fourth book of his *Speculum historiae de gestis regum Angliae*, provides just over 500 words on Edith's qualities and attainments which he found in his abbey's copy of *Vita*. It is clear on stylistic grounds that, as usual with him, he mostly copied verbatim.

This reduces the loss to 700 words which cannot be recovered. It may be supposed that they concerned Edith's brothers and possibly sisters, presumably the four brothers who occur elsewhere in the tract, Harold, Tostig, Gyrth and Leofwine, and just possibly the nun Gunhild, who shortly after the Conquest — but probably after this part of *Vita* had been written — took refuge at Saint-Omer, the presumed home of the writer. Twice later in the tract, when mentioning Gyrth, the encomiast refers back to earlier treatment, presumably in the lost chapter; but Leofwine is named without comment. Harold and Tostig come in for fuller treatment in chapter 5. The brothers Swegen and Wulfnoth, the one unworthy and dead, the other a hostage in Normandy, seem to have been entirely ignored by the writer, presumably on Edith's instructions. If the sisters Gunhild and Ælfgifu were also omitted, it may have been likewise because they played no part in the story. The loss of more than half of chapter 2 is all the more unfortunate since the missing passage might have helped to explain the enigmatic poem which concludes the chapter and disguises most of the principal actors as rivers and birds.

The Godwins do not feature much in other saints' lives. There are some references in *Vita Wulfstani*, the life of St Wulfstan bishop of Worcester (1062–95)[12]; but the family had no reputation for religion. Indeed, it was generally regarded as a despoiler of the church, although there were few great families at the time which did not give with one hand while taking away with the other. Most dynasties considered the church to be unconscionably greedy for lands. What a dying father gave to atone for his sins, his sons did their best to obstruct or recover.

Documentary evidence is not plentiful. The wills of none of the Godwins have survived, nor have other legal instruments. The diplomas of the kings, however, shed a little light on the position of members of the family at the royal court.[13] For their landed wealth, Domesday Book (1086) is a wonderful record, although at some considerable distance.[14]

The early nineteenth-century pioneers of modern historiography, Sharon Turner, *The History of the Anglo-Saxons*, 3 vols, 3rd edn, 1820, Francis Palgrave, *A History of the Anglo-Saxons*, 1832, J.M. Lappenberg, translated by Benjamin Thorpe, *A History of England under the Anglo-Saxon Kings*, 2 vols, 1845, and J.M. Kemble, *The Saxons in England*, 2 vols, 1849, provided no index to their works. On the other hand, E.A. Freeman's *The History of the Norman Conquest of England*, in 5 volumes, the first of which appeared in 1867, is fully indexed in a sixth volume as well as in some of the earlier volumes. Freeman revised his work incessantly, and footnotes spilled into appendices. The sheer length is daunting. But this Oxford scholar's magisterial contribution to our knowledge, although it was mercilessly, and at what now seems excessive length, criticized by J.H. Round, remains the basic work on the Godwins and cannot be neglected by any of his successors. Freeman was a Victorian liberal with strong prejudices and some obvious technical faults. But his general view of English history has in part come into fashion again after the rather illiberal twentieth century. The next standard general work on the period is F.M. Stenton's *Anglo-Saxon England* (1943, 1947, 1971). This is academic scholarship at its best, technically excellent and cool in tone. Since then, the secondary literature has proliferated. Renewed study of Domesday Book, facilitated by new editions, indexes and the use of the computer, has inspired much of it. And women's studies have given history a new slant and topic. Most of the modern monographs provide up-to-date bibliographies.

Two studies of Harold Godwinson deserve special mention: H.R. Loyn's lecture in 1966, *Harold son of Godwin*, and Ian W. Walker's *Harold, the last Anglo-Saxon King*. The former offers a brief but perceptive view of his subject. The latter is a fairly long work, fully illustrated, which provides a thorough and careful investigation of Harold's career. Pauline Stafford's study of Edith, Godwin's daughter, together with Emma, her mother-in-law, is especially interesting for its sociological approach and feminist viewpoint. *Queen Emma and Queen Edith* (1997) is also erudite and comprehensive.

At the other end of the spectrum are the avowed works of fiction by modern authors. These can be useful for their unrestrained views of the events and the *dramatis personae*. They can also be entertaining. The prolific novelist Sir Edward Bulwer Lytton, Bart. (first baron Lytton) published his *Harold: the last of the Saxon Kings* in 1848. Aged 45 and a novelist of over twenty years' experience, he wrote the book in three weeks spent mainly in the library of his friend the Rt. Hon. C.T. D'Eyncourt, M.P., to whom he dedicated it. The Norman Conquest, he thought, 'was our Trojan War, an epoch beyond which our learning seldom induces our imagination to ascend'. His narrative has such drive and fluency that, despite a good number of archaic words and phrases, the reader is increasingly captivated by the story. And, apart from the unhistorical Edith Swan-neck, Bulwer Lytton aimed at telling a story as faithful as possible to the sources, some of which he identifies in his notes.

In 1877 Alfred (Lord) Tennyson, the poet and a nephew of D'Eyncourt, published his *Harold, a drama*, a verse play in five acts. He dedicated this in return to H.E. the Rt. Hon. Lord Lytton, viceroy and governor-general of India, the son of Bulwer-Lytton, to whose *Harold* he acknowledged much help. Indeed, the virginal Edith Swan-neck reappears. This drama cannot be considered one of Tennyson's more successful works. And it seems never to have been performed.

In every way more attractive is Hope Muntz's *The Golden Warrior: the story of Harold and William*, which in 1949 she dedicated to the Rt. Hon. Winston Churchill, O.M. 'in remembrance of 1940'. Composing in short chapters in fluent and often pithy English, she claims to have made use of legends

THE GODWINS

and tradition only when they enrich the story and do not conflict with the known facts. She acknowledges that Harold's love for Edith Swan-neck is one of the enrichments — 'but at no time has history been intentionally falsified'. The claim is largely true; and the book makes pleasant and easy reading.

The last of the novels, Julian Rathbone's *The last English King*, published in 1997, is very different from the others. In his prefatory note he acknowledges three sorts of possible anachronism: the unintentional ('fair game for swots, letter-writers, anoraks and so on'), the composition in modern prose with its 'bad language'; and the references to later times. The last are unobtrusive. The factual errors are not of much importance. The coarse language attributed to the 'royals' is incongruous only in the case of the convent-educated, scholarly and refined Queen Edith. And the erotic scenes are unexpected ornaments. More important is the drastic and, of course, unsubstantiated re-interpretation of the characters and their relationships. Edward is suffering from diabetes. His queen, Edith, has been raped by her father, Earl Godwin, and seduced by her brother, Earl Harold. She and Harold remain close. She solaces herself with toy-boys. Tostig is the king's lover. Much of this is good fun; and some episodes are very amusing. The book can be read for pleasure if not for historical information. And there is much to ponder. For example, did the author of *Vita Ædwardi Regis* get it all wrong?

It must be recognized that the original sources for the history of the Godwins are not only scanty but also for the most part heavily biased. The English and the Norman views can hardly be reconciled. Moreover, the twelfth-century English historians, such as William of Malmesbury, owing to the thinness of the English sources, had perforce to accept in the main the Norman story. There is, for example, no English account of the battle of Hastings. Even the book in praise of the Godwins, *Vita Ædwardi Regis*, is not whole-heartedly on the side of Harold: his brother Tostig looms always in the background. Hence many episodes remain both obscure and controversial. The inequality in the evidence has not prevented a partisanship in the interpretation of the events and persons that has persisted throughout the historiography. Freeman was badly torn: his sympathies were with Harold but he could not deny the greatness of William. If all these features make the writing of a history of the Godwins difficult, they also make it instructive. There are always problems to be solved. And, most important of all, the people involved are worth writing about. They are all flawed heroes and heroines in a northern saga.

Notes

Full details of publications cited appear in the Bibliography.

1. See *English Historical Documents*, ed. David C. Douglas, vol. i, *c.* 500–1042, ed. Dorothy Whitelock (1968), vol. ii, 1042–1189, ed. D.C. Douglas and G.W. Greenaway (2nd edn, 1981). E. van Houts, 'Historical Writing', *A Companion to the Anglo-Norman World*, ed. C. Harper-Bill and E. van Houts (2003), pp. 103–21. For Æthelred's reign, Simon Keynes, *The Diplomas of King Æthelred 'the Unready', 978–1016* (1980), pp. 274–84. For Cnut's reign, M.K. Lawson, *Cnut, the Danes in England in the early eleventh century*, The Medieval World (1993); Longman, Harlow, pp. 247–70. For Edward the Confessor's reign, Frank Barlow, *Edward the Confessor*, Yale edn 1997, pp. 337–55.

2. *The Anglo-Saxon Chronicle: a collaborative edition in 23 vols*, vol. 6, *MS. D*, ed. G.P. Gubbin (Cambridge, 1996); vol. 10, *The Abingdon Chronicle, AD 956–1066*, ed. P.W. Conner (1996). See also D. Whitelock in *EHD*, i. 109–10, 135–235; ii. 103–215, separately printed as *The Anglo-Saxon Chronicle*, ed. Dorothy Whitelock with David C. Douglas and Susie I. Tucker (1961); Körner, pp. 1–46; and Stafford, pp. 6–9.

3. *The* Gesta Normannorum Ducum *of William of Jumièges*, ed. and trans. by E.M.C. van Houts (Oxford Medieval Texts, 1992–5) [*GND*].

4. *The* Gesta Guillelmi *of William of Poitiers*, ed. and trans. by R.H.C. Davis and M. Chibnall (Oxford Medieval Texts, 1998) [*GG*].

5. *The* Carmen de Hastingae Proelio *of Guy bishop of Amiens*, ed. and trans. by F. Barlow (Oxford Medieval Texts, 1999) [*Carmen*].
6. Ordericus Vitalis, *Historia Ecclesiastica*, ed. and trans. by M. Chibnall (Oxford Medieval Texts (1969–80)) [*OV*].
7. Used here are *The Bayeux Tapestry: a History and Description*, by F.R. Fowke (1898), and *The Bayeux Tapestry: a Comprehensive Survey*, by Sir Frank Stenton *et al.* (1957). Continuous folding editions are also useful.
8. R. Dodwell in *The Observer*, supplement, 31 October 1965, pp. 21–2.
9. Snorri Sturluson, *Heimskringla*, ed. S. Laing (2nd edn, 1880); 'Saga of Olaf Haroldson', in Snorre Sturluson, *Heimskringla*, trans. by S. Laing (London, 1906); *Harald Sigurdsson, King Harald's Saga*, trans. M. Magnusson and H. Pálsson (Penguin Classics, 1966); Saxo Grammaticus, *Hist. Danicae, libri XVI*, Monumenta Germ. Hist., ser. xxix.; *Gesta Danorum of Saxo Grammaticus*, ed. J. Olrik and H. Raeder (Copenhagen, 1931); *Gesta Hammaburgensis Ecclesiae of Adam of Bremen*, ed. J.M. Lappenberg (2nd edn, Hanover, 1876).
10. *Encomium Emmae Reginae*, ed. A. Campbell (Royal Hist. Soc., Camden 3rd ser., lxxii, 1949) [*Encomium Emmae*]. See also Stafford, pp. 28–40. She thinks it was aimed only at Harold I, who was already dead.
11. *The Life of King Edward who rests at Westminster*, ed. and trans. by F. Barlow (Oxford Medieval Texts, 2nd edn, 1992). [*Vita*]. See also Stafford, pp. 40–8.
12. *The* Vita Wulfstani *of William of Malmesbury*, ed. by R.R. Darlington (Royal Hist. Soc., Camden 3rd ser., xl, 1928 [*Vita Wulfstani*].
13. J.M. Kemble, *Codex Diplomaticus Aevi Saxonici*, 6 vols (1839–48) [*KCD*]; P.H. Sawyer, *Anglo-Saxon Charters, an Annotated List and Bibliography* (Royal Hist. Soc., Guides and Handbooks, 1968).
14. There are several modern editions. One, with excellent photographic reproductions and translations, is the county by county volumes of Alecto Historical Editions. [*DB*].

Table 1 KINGS OF ENGLAND
Anglo-Saxon line

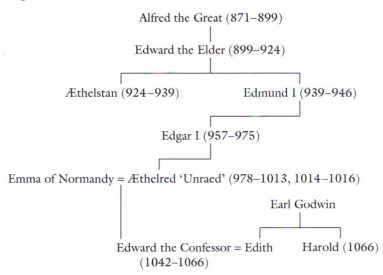

Alfred the Great (871–899)

Edward the Elder (899–924)

Æthelstan (924–939)   Edmund I (939–946)

Edgar I (957–975)

Emma of Normandy = Æthelred 'Unraed' (978–1013, 1014–1016)

Earl Godwin

Edward the Confessor = Edith   Harold (1066)
(1042–1066)

Table 2 KINGS OF ENGLAND
Danish line

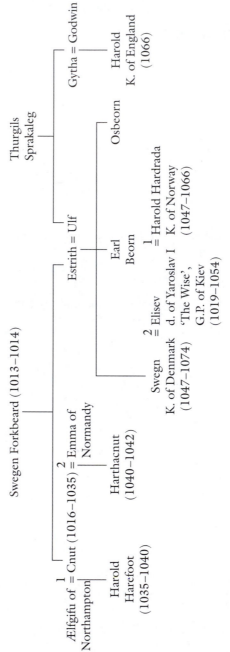

Table 3 EARL GODWIN'S ANCESTORS
A simplified genealogy based on A. Anscombe and L.W. Barlow

Æthelwulf
sub-king of Kent 825
king of the West Saxons 839–58

Æthelred I
king of the West Saxons 865–71

Alfred the Great
king of the West Saxons 871–99

Æthelhelm
? ealdorman of Wilts
died 898

English kings to 1066

Æthelfrith
ealdorman occ. 901–24

Eadric
ealdorman occ. 925–49

Æthelweard
'the historian' ealdorman of the
western provinces occ. 956–98

Æthelmaer Cild
ealdorman of the western
provinces occ. 1005–15

Wulfnoth Cild
thegn of Sussex
occ. 1009, died in or before 1014

Æthelnoth
archbp of Canterbury
1020–1038

Godwin
earl of Wessex
died 1053

? Ælfwig
abbot of New Minster
1063–6

? Æthelflaed = Toki

THE GODWINS

Table 4 THE GODWINS

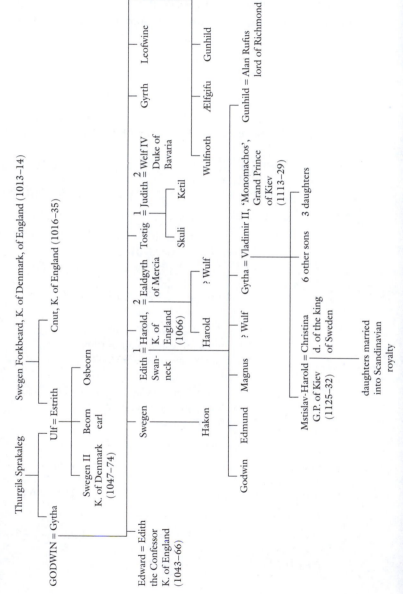

chapter 1

THE FAMILY'S ORIGINS AND GODWIN'S EARLY YEARS

S ince Godwin's daughter, Queen Edith, was the fruit of the union of two noble families, one English, one Danish, it might be expected that the tract she commissioned to eulogise her family, *Vita Ædwardi Regis*, would pay considerable attention to her forebears. In the prefatory poem, indeed, the Muse bids the author write in praise of Edith and her husband the king and tell how her father Godwin, 'esteemed for his respect and loyalty (*fidei pietate cluentem*)', founded four comital lines in England.[1] These are probably those of Harold, Tostig, Gyrth and Leofwine, for the disreputable eldest son, Swegen, is not mentioned in *Vita*. And, remarkably in this context, Godwin's own ancestors, like those of his wife, are completely ignored. Chapter i.1 begins abruptly with the Danish conqueror Cnut (who had established his position in England in 1016), choosing Godwin from among the English nobles as his favourite, taking him with him to put down a rebellion in Denmark (?1019), giving him his sister as wife, appointing him an ealdorman, and making him the power behind the throne.[2] But we have to wait for the third poem for Godwin to be described as 'blessed in his ancestral stock and fortunate in his dutiful offspring'.[3] And then, although we hear much of the children, we are told nothing of the ancestral stock. There is massive evasion here. Not only is Godwin's background totally ignored, but also his wife is probably incorrectly identified. Gytha was more likely the daughter of Thurgils Sprakaleg and sister of the Danish jarl Ulf who married Estrith, Cnut's sister.[4] Moreover, although she was still alive in 1066, she is not named in *Vita* and rarely mentioned. The reasons for these silences, all the more remarkable since Edith clearly loved and revered her father, are discussed below.[5]

The encomiast's view of Godwin's background may, however, be encoded in a poem he provides on the earl's triumphant return from exile in 1052.[6] He likens Godwin's relations with King Edward to David's with King Saul as told in the Bible (I Samuel xvi–xxxi). David, the son of Jesse and the fourteenth generation from Abraham, became the first king of the Judaean dynasty in Israel and a direct ancestor of Jesus Christ (Matthew i. 1–17). But, although of distinguished lineage and with a successful, if chequered, career and illustrious descendants, David started life as a poor lad, a youngest son and a shepherd, who made his career first by his skill as a harpist and then as a soldier against the Philistines. Since, however, the encomiast's main point is that Godwin spared Edward's life when it was in his power to kill, just as David spared Saul's because of his reverence for the Lord's anointed, other concordances cannot be taken for granted.

There is good evidence that Godwin's father was named Wulfnoth (*Cild*),[7] a name Godwin gave to one, perhaps the youngest, of his sons; and there is a 'confused and doubtful' later tradition that Ælfwig (Ælfwy), abbot of New Minster, Winchester (1063–6), who was killed in the battle of Hastings, was Godwin's brother.[8] There also seems to have been a sister, Æthelflaed.[9] The Victorian historian E.A. Freeman was a great admirer of Godwin and, when writing and revising his massive *History of the Norman Conquest* in the 1870s, was much interested in his ancestry. But he was doubtful which of two possible

Wulfnoths his father was. Yet the Godwins' massive estates in Sussex, as shown in Domesday Book (1086) — the family held over 1,200 hides, about one third of the shire — are indisputable evidence that Wulfnoth was the South Saxon thegn.[10] And it was left to Alfred Anscombe in 1913 and Lundie W. Barlow in 1955, by treating Wulfnoth as the son of Æthelmaer, ealdorman of the western provinces, and tracing the descent of some estates, especially Compton in Westbourne Hundred in Sussex, to take the pedigree back through seven generations to Æthelwulf, the king of the West Saxons who died in 858 and was a descendant of the sixth-century Cerdic, the founder of the dynasty.[11] This pedigree, even if mistaken, is of the right type. The Anglo-Saxon kings mostly married into the English nobility, and much of the aristocracy was inter-related. A rival medieval view, that Godwin was of low birth, an upstart, although it would explain the obscurity of his background, seems inherently unlikely.[12]

The main difficulty with the pedigree created by Anscombe and Barlow is that seven generations with almost all the family names beginning with Æthel/Alf (noble) mutate suddenly to Wulfnoth and Godwin. Barlow suggested that if Compton was inherited by Wulfnoth through his mother, royal descent was through her. But there were some exceptions in the nomenclature with younger children, and fashions could change. Also it is likely that there were some drastic disturbances in the family's fortunes during the reign of Æthelred II, 'the Unready', when viking raids made deep inroads into the kingdom, Danish kings aimed at conquest and for a short time succeeded, and disloyalty to Æthelred was rife.

There can be no doubt that Æthelred was an incompetent ruler. His punning nickname, Æthelred Unraed (noble counsel: no counsel) points to his foolishness; and there was much complaint of the absence of good justice and sound government. It is true that he faced enormous difficulties. But the successes of some of his predecessors, such as Alfred, and of his own son Edmund Ironside at the end of the reign, show what a wise and resolute king could achieve. The way in which Æthelred had succeeded to the throne (after the murder of his elder stepbrother, Edward 'the Martyr') and then his erratic conduct of affairs destroyed confidence in his leadership and eventually led to treason. Moreover, by marrying in 1002 Emma, the daughter of Richard I count of Normandy and the grand-daughter of a viking adventurer, and by recruiting viking forces, such as Thorkell Havi and his 45 ships in 1012 and Olaf Haroldsson, the future king of Norway and saint, in 1014, Æthelred helped to blur English ethnic loyalties and make it easier for English nobles to desert him for successful Scandinavian invaders.

In 1005–6 a palace revolution seems to have occurred. Several influential noblemen, including Ealdorman Æthelmaer, Wulfnoth's supposed father, disappear from the royal court and the ascent of the Mercian Eadric Streona (the Acquisitor) and his family begins.[13] Eadric became notorious for his greed for lands, for his treachery, and for his involvement in murders. He also presided over a period of almost farcical disasters. In 1008 Æthelred ordered a fleet to be built; and the next year some 300 ships were assembled at Sandwich in Kent, 'the most famous of all English ports',[14] in order to intercept a threatened viking invasion. At this time Brihtric, a brother of Eadric Streona, denounced Wulfnoth Cild of the South Saxons, probably Æthelmaer's son and Godwin's father, to the king, accusing him of some unspecified crime. Whereupon Wulfnoth rebelled, seduced twenty ships, presumably his or his father's contribution to the fleet, and ravaged the south coast. Brihtric then took eighty ships against him, intending his capture or death. But a tempest drove them ashore, where Wulfnoth burnt them. This diversion or destruction of a third of the English fleet caused such disarray that the king and his leading men left

Sandwich while the remaining ships were transferred to London. As a result, in August viking forces were able to land unopposed in Kent. In 1013 Æthelmaer also defected: with 'all the western thegns' he surrendered to King Swegen at Bath and gave hostages.[15]

All that we know for certain about Wulfnoth and Æthelmaer's subsequent careers is that the former was dead by 25 June 1014 when the atheling Athelstan, King Æthelred's eldest son, made his will and died, and that Æthelmaer died soon after.[16] We should note, however, the fate of the hostages Æthelmaer had given in 1013. These, after King Swegen's death on 3 February 1014 and Æthelred's temporary recovery of the throne, were mutilated by Swegen's son, Cnut — he had their hands, noses and ears cut off — and put ashore before he left England for Denmark.[17] It is just possible, although perhaps unlikely, especially in view of Godwin's adherence to Cnut two years later, that Wulfnoth was one of the unfortunate hostages. We are on firmer ground in thinking that Æthelred had punished Wulfnoth in 1009 and his father in 1013 for their defections by confiscation of property. In any case the family was in dire trouble. In 1014, however, a helping hand was offered when the atheling Athelstan in his will, which his reinstated father ratified, restored to Godwin, Wulfnoth's son, the land at Compton (Sussex) which his father had owned.[18] The bequest shows that in 1014 Godwin was in Athelstan's good books and maybe an adherent of the atheling's warrior brother, Edmund Ironside.

The date of Godwin's birth can only be conjectured. As he died in 1053 and is unlikely to have lived long after sixty, he was probably born not far before 993. And as he was certainly adult in 1018–19 a much later date is precluded. If Godwin was indeed born about 993 in Sussex, he probably spent his youth on the fringe of the areas most heavily disturbed by viking raids. These had started again with Olaf Trygvason's attack on Kent in 991, taken a more serious turn with the invasion of Danish armies under the brothers Thorkell the Tall and Heming in 1009–12,[19] and become overwhelming when Swegen Forkbeard, king of Denmark, invaded in 1013 and forced the English royal family to take refuge in Normandy.[20] The invaders from Denmark or Normandy found entry easier through Kent or up Southampton Water than through Sussex, enclosed as it was by the Downs and the forest of Andredsweald. But the shire was ravaged in at least 994, 998 and 1009.[21] It would also have had to contribute to the large sums of money which local communities and the royal government raised in order to buy the invaders off, as well as bear the cost of King Æthelred's several attempts to create a defensive navy. They were hard times for all.

Until 1013 the main purpose of the raids was to collect provisions and loot; and what the vikings could not carry away they burnt or destroyed. The damage was, of course, patchy. Even armies to be numbered in thousands, while cutting a swathe through the countryside and occasionally sacking a town or borough, left even larger areas untouched. Nevertheless the kingdom as a whole was greatly disturbed. For the contemporary, or near contemporary, chronicler, a monk of Abingdon Abbey in Berkshire, it was a story of English ineptitude and cowardice, of royal irresolution and aristocratic treachery, with even the rare heroics ending in disaster and with no English military successes before Edmund Ironside's unsustained victories in the spring of 1016. For Wulfstan the Homilist it was a time of shame. Even more disgraceful, he thought, than the ignominy inflicted by the heathen on the Christians, by the pirates and their slaves on the English nobility, was the acceptance of their insults by the English: thegns watching their own womenfolk being raped, sometimes by a dozen soldiers in turn; people just watching while two or three seamen drove throngs of Christians to their ships to be sold as slaves.[22]

The survivors from such conditions, men like Edward the Confessor, women like Edward's mother, Emma of Normandy, were those who swam with the tide. Godwin's career and his later reputation for patience and diplomacy do not suggest a reckless youth.[23] Although he would have been a horseman and familiar with weapons, practised in the art of hunting, and was, when necessary, physically resourceful, he seems always to have yielded to force and avoided battle. There is in fact no evidence that he had had any military experience before he accompanied King Cnut to Denmark early in his reign, and then he did not necessarily get involved in any fighting. All the same, the encomiast believed that not only his prudence in counsel but also his experience in warfare recommended him to Cnut.[24] And, although Freeman's conjecture that 'Godwin was a young warrior whose services under Edmund [in 1014] entitled him to a restitution of the lands forfeited by his father'[25] may be an exaggeration, it cannot be doubted that Godwin as a boy and youth had lived through dangerous times. Much of the half-remembered story of those years could, however, best be left untold by the chroniclers and especially by an encomiast of the family.

Godwin escaped Cnut's initial purge of the leading members of the English aristocracy, perhaps because of his adroitness, possibly because of his reputation for loyalty. Queen Emma's encomiast believed that Cnut 'loved those whom he heard to have fought previously for Edmund [Ironside] faithfully and without deceit'. It may also have been Godwin's control of Sussex and its ports which recommended him.[26] And after Cnut's general acceptance as king and the elimination of most of the possible dissidents, began a new and for some eighteen years more settled era, a time of growing prosperity for Godwin and his family. The slate was largely wiped clean. It also saw the beginnings of an improvement in the climate, the start of a warmer period, in which the increasing profits from agriculture enabled the population to grow. The whole kingdom became richer.

Edith's encomiast's view of these years, doubtless reflecting that of his patron, is most interesting.[27] He regarded Edward (the Confessor) as the true heir to Æthelred. When that king's wife, Emma, was pregnant with him, all the men of the country took an oath that if she produced a son, 'they would await in him their lord and king who would rule over the whole race of the English'. They had indeed to wait for some time; and the encomiast explained the Danish invasions as God's punishment for the (unspecified) sins of the English people, so that Edward's eventual accession to the throne in 1042 was the people's jubilee, that is to say the year in which they recovered their freedom and reverted to their original master. The Danes were barbarians, ravagers and oppressors; but Cnut, who obtained the kingdom 'as a result of the vicissitudes of war', is not identified as a Dane or awarded either praise or blame. His sons, Harold Harefoot and Harthacnut, who ruled in turn after his death, are not mentioned until in chapter i.3 Harold comes into the story in connection with the quarrel between Godwin and Robert of Jumièges, archbishop of Canterbury, in 1051, when he is called a bastard and 'an arrogant fellow of bad character'.[28] Edith obviously had no love of Danes.

The *Vita* also takes little interest in Edith's mother, Gytha, and mother-in-law, Emma. Neither is named. The former is noticed as Godwin's bride, as accompanying him into exile in 1051, and as saying goodbye to her son Tostig when he left England in 1066.[29] Emma is mentioned only in connection with the birth of Edward;[30] and it is not stated that after Æthelred's death she married Cnut and had a second brood. Edith may have regarded both these formidable ladies as rivals for control over her husband, Edward the Confessor.

If Godwin was indeed born about 993 and the Wulfnoth who was dead by 1014 was his father, and the Æthelmaer Cild who died in the following year his grandfather, he would have inherited in his early manhood such family estates as remained. It should be noticed that his royal master, Cnut, is thought to have been born *c.* 995; and the relative youth of both in 1016 may have helped the mutual attraction. Edward the Confessor, his future son-in-law, was born about 1005, a decade after the other two.

Godwin was quickly rewarded by Cnut.[31] By 1018 he had received an earldom, perhaps the ancestral Wessex or part of it, and in 1019 marriage to the king's sister-in-law Gytha. This girl, a sister of the Danish Jarl Ulf and a daughter of the famous Thurgils Sprakaleg (who was reputed to be descended from a bear), must have been quite young in 1019, for she was still active in 1066. She clearly became important in her husband's life and developed into a remarkable woman. She reared at least six sons: Swegen, Harold, Tostig, Gyrth, Leofwine and Wulfnoth, and three daughters, Edith, Gunhild and Ælfgifu.[32] Godwin, however, attracted legends. And in the twelfth century William of Malmesbury believed that Cnut's 'sister' was the earl's first of two wives.[33] She produced a son who was very proud of a horse his grandfather gave him. But the steed carried the boy into the river Thames where the rider drowned. She herself, as punishment for her wickedness, was killed by a bolt of lightning. Her crime was her purchasing large numbers of slaves in England, especially young and beautiful girls, in order to export them to Denmark. From this trade she made great wealth. After her death Godwin married another woman, whose family William could not discover, who bore him six (correctly named) sons. The chronicler then tells of the fate of Harold, Wulfnoth, Swegen and Tostig.

At the end of the twelfth century Godwin is featured in Walter Map's collection of amusing historical anecdotes, *De Nugis Curialium* (The Trifles of Courtiers).[34] The son of a cowherd, Godwin impresses King Æthelred who had gone astray when hunting and sought hospitality at their cottage. Æthelred takes him into his service and promotes him to greatness, making him earl of Gloucester. So crafty was Godwin that he obtained the nunnery of Berkeley and the manor of Bosham by guile. He got the first by insinuating an attractive nephew into the house who so debauched the nuns that the king dissolved the community and gave the estate to Godwin. Domesday Book (1086) alludes to this business. The Gloucestershire jurors declared that Earl Godwin bought Woodchester from Azur and gave it to his wife Gytha so that she could live from it when she stayed at Berkeley. But she did not want to eat anything from it because of the destruction of the abbey.[35]

Godwin acquired Bosham by a trick. He said to the arch-bishop of Canterbury, whose manor it was, 'Lord, do you give me Bosham?' And when the startled prelate answered questioningly, 'I give you Bosham?', the earl and his men fell at his feet, kissed them and gave him profuse thanks for his gift. They then hurried off and took possession of it. Even more surprisingly, we are told that Godwin not only put down piracy in all the English ports, but also, 'aflame with the love of war', went on a Crusade against the Saracens.

Walter Map continues: when Cnut invaded, Godwin and Edmund Ironside faced the invader at Deerhurst. But the battle was avoided by substituting a duel between the two leaders. After Edmund's death Cnut became such a tyrant that Godwin became his pitiless and cruel enemy and fought against him until Cnut made a fraudulent peace with him, sending him to Denmark with sealed letters ordering his execution. But after opening the letters on the advice of his chaplain, Brand, he substituted an order to put Godwin, his sister's husband, earl of York and lord of Lincoln, Nottingham, Leicester, Chester, Huntingdon, Northampton, Gloucester and Hereford, in total charge of the kingdom of Denmark. At this point Map's story of Godwin breaks off. These legends — and there were others too — show that Godwin became something of a folk hero in England, but, because of his denigration by Norman writers, a rather sinister figure, insinuating and crafty. Waltham Abbey, his son Harold's great foundation, remembered him as deceitful.

It is noticeable that the elder sons of Godwin and Gytha were given Danish names. The family was presumably bilingual and must be considered Anglo–Danish, not Anglo–Saxon. In fact Godwin's three eldest sons and one of his daughters were given Danish names, presumably because their mother was Danish and Godwin was wholeheartedly in this new allegiance. A different explanation, however, was offered by the eldest son, Swegn. According to Heming's Worcester cartulary, under Shropshire which was part of Swegn's earldom in 1043–6, this arrogant fellow maintained that King Cnut, not Godwin, was his true father. However, his mother indignantly denied it, even on oath in an assembly of Wessex noblewomen she convened.[36] Favourable to Swegn's claim are his possession of a name which ran in the Danish royal family, his constant behaviour among the Godwins as an outsider, and his apparent total exclusion from *Vita*, the family's saga. Moreover, if Cnut was indeed Gytha's lover, the favours he granted Godwin are more understandable.[37] The truth of the matter cannot, of course, be determined. We simply notice that the preference for Danish personal names continued in the third generation. Harold's and Tostig's children mostly had Scandinavian names, and Tostig's two boys settled happily in Norway. The family's encomiast regarded Godwin as a good father. In the education of his children he paid attention especially to those arts which would prepare them to be a strength and help to future rulers and, concentrating his attention on Edith, who was educated in Wilton nunnery, describes her piety, good manners, expertise in embroidery and other arts, skill in Latin prose and verse, and ability to speak 'French', Danish and Irish as though they were her mother tongues.[38] What he understood by Irish is uncertain. If he wrote in detail of the education of the sons, this could have been in the lost parts of this chapter (i.2). It is not impossible, as with King Alfred and with Godwin's supposed great-grandfather, Æthelweard 'the historian', that the boys were given some literary education. Harold was believed to have had some books, including one on falconry.[39] But in fact no son entered the church and the five eldest became soldiers. They would have been trained almost exclusively in hunting and fighting. We would probably know more about these boys if we had chapter 2 of *Vita* in full.[40]

Notes

1. *Vita*, pp. 4–9.
2. Ibid., pp. 8–11.
3. Ibid., pp. 26–9. This is a very obscure poem. Queen Edith is introduced rather awkwardly and it is uncertain who the four children are or what they are supposed to have done. The baffling imagery has been studied by Rhona Beare, 'Swallows and Barnacle Geese', *Notes and Queries*, ccxliii (1998), p. 5. See also below, pp. 119–21.
4. *FNC*, i. app. EEE, 'The exploits and marriage of Godwine', pp. 743–7; Lawson, *Cnut*, p. 188, accepts without comment that she was Cnut's sister.
5. See p. 30.
6. *Vita*, pp. 44–6.
7. *FNC*, i. app. ZZ, 'The origin of Earl Godwine', pp. 719–31; cf. i. app. MM, 'Wulfnoth of Sussex'. The exact significance of *Cild*, which normally means 'child', when attached to an aristocrat's name, is disputed. Cf. *FNC*, i. 664; iv. 759. B. Thorpe, in his glossary to his edition of *ASC* (Rolls ser., 1861), ii. 321, considers it a title nearly synonymous with atheling and one given to the younger branches of royalty and higher families. He cites Wulfnoth Cild as an example. It is probably better regarded as a step-down from atheling (*clito* in Latin), which usually means 'throneworthy': see below, p. 82.

8. *The Heads of Religious Houses, England and Wales, 940–1216*, ed. D. Knowles, C.N.L. Brooke, V.C.M. London (Cambridge, 1972), p. 81.
9. Lundie W. Barlow, 'The antecedents of Earl Godwine of Wessex', *New England Historical and Genealogical Register*, lxi (1957), 32.
10. *FNC*, 'The origin of Earl Godwine', i. 719–31; A. Williams, 'Land and power in the eleventh century: the estates of Harold Godwineson', *ANS*, iii (1981), 176–7.
11. A. Anscombe, 'The pedigree of Earl Godwin', *Trans. R. Hist. Soc.*, 3rd ser., vii (1913), 129–50; Lundie W. Barlow, 'The antecedents of Earl Godwine of Wessex', *New England Historical and Genealogical Register*, lxi (1957), 30–8.
12. *FNC*, i. app. MM and ZZ; C.E. Wright, *The Cultivation of Saga in Anglo-Saxon England* (Edinburgh, 1939), pp. 213–36. See also below, p. 31–2.
13. Keynes, pp. 209–13.
14. *Encomium Emmae*, p. 21.
15. *ASC, s.a.*
16. *EHD*, i. 548–50. His will and death are dated by Keynes, p. 267. But cf. Barlow, *Edward*, pp. 30–1, n. 3.
17. *ASC, s.a.* 1014.
18. As above, n. 16.
19. *ASC, s.a.*
20. Ibid.
21. Ibid.
22. Wulfstan, *Sermo Lupi ad Anglos*, ed. D. Whitelock (2nd edn, 1952). *EHD*, i. 855–9, at pp. 857–8.
23. *Vita*, pp. 10–11, 32–7, 42–3. His encomiast does, however, refer to his martial courage (*virtutis militia*) and have him recalling his former valour and the many feats of his early manhood (*memor antiquae virtutis et tot laborum pristinae iuventutis*), ibid., pp. 40–1.
24. *Vita*, pp. 8–9.
25. *FNC*, i. 730.
26. *Encomium Emmae*, pp. 30–1; Williams (as above, n. 10), p. 187.
27. *Vita*, pp. 8–15.
28. Ibid., pp. 32–5.
29. Ibid., pp. 10–11, 36–7, 82–3.
30. Ibid., pp. 12–13.

31. Godwin first attests as *dux* a (not completely authentic) charter of Cnut dated 1018. It is in favour of Bishop Buruhwold of Cornwall and concerns estates in Devon and Cornwall: K. 728, S. 951. See *FNC*, i, app. AAA, 'The West-Saxon earldom', pp. 731–3.

32. For Godwin's children, see *FNC*, ii, app., note F, pp. 568–71. Ælfgifu, who is named in Domesday Book, appears unnamed in Eadmer's account of Harold's promises to William of Normandy in 1064–5, *Historia Novorum*, pp. 7–8. She was to have been married to a Norman nobleman, but died. She could possibly have been the Ælfgyva of the Bayeux Tapestry; see below, p. 100–1. Although it is usually assumed that Edith, because she was the one chosen to marry the king, was the eldest daughter, her English rather than Danish name raises doubts.

33. *GR*, i. 245.

34. *De Nugis Curialium*, distinct. V, caps iii–iv, ed. T. Wright, The Camden Soc. (1850), pp. 199–209; trans. M.R. James, Hon. Soc. of Cymmrodorion, record ser., no. ix (1923), pp. 228–41; *Vita Haroldi*, trans. Swanton, pp. 3–4, where the story of his being sent to Denmark to be killed also appears.

35. *DB*, i. 164.

36. *Hemingi Chartularium*, ed. T. Hearne (Oxford, 1723), I, 275.

37. Mrs Patricia A. Millward wrote to urge me to take Swegn's claim more seriously.

38. *Vita*, pp. 10–11, 22–5. For a further testimonial to her scholastic attainments, see her Winchester obituary, below, pp. 161–2.

39. C.H. Haskins, 'King Harold's books', *EHR*, xxxvii (1922), 398–400; *Studies in the History of Medieval Science*, 2nd edn (1927), pp. 28, 346–8.

40. See above, pp. 12–13 and below, 119–21.

chapter 2

GODWIN UNDER THE DANISH KINGS, 1016–1042

B y adhering to Cnut in 1016 and serving him faithfully, Godwin either restored or founded the family's fortune. As an ealdorman somewhere in greater Wessex — and by the end of the reign he was titled ealdorman of Wessex[1] — he came into possession of the estates which had been royal demesne; and these he could increase by exploiting both his local position and his favour with the king. Although, except in *Vita Ædwardi Regis*, he never enjoyed an unambiguous favourable reputation, he fared much better than Eadric Streona ('the Acquisitor'). Godwin may well have been just as rapacious, but his almost continuous service to four consecutive kings suppressed criticism. He was of course an opportunist with a good eye for the winner, and through his timely support securing victory for his candidate, a deed which earned him rewards. All the English nobles were involved in these high-risk operations: the prudent Godwin just did better than the rest.

According to *Vita*, Cnut, after observing and testing Godwin's abilities, made him not only an ealdorman (*dux*) but also *bajulus* of almost all the kingdom.[2] *Bajulus*, which is cognate with *baillivus*, a bailiff, and signified some position of responsibility, cannot be equated with any established or recognizable office. It can be compared with the chief justiciarship which developed later under the Angevin kings of England. Godwin became the senior ealdorman, or earl as he can now be termed, the most intimate with the king, in some ways his deputy. According to *Vita*: 'What he decreed should be written was written, what he decreed should be erased was erased.' The qualities which most impressed the king were his intelligence (*prudentia*), his steadfastness, his strength and courage, and his eloquence. These are, indeed, useful abilities in a subordinate. Moreover, the encomiast continues, Godwin was a model governor. Rather than acting proudly, he became a father figure to all good men. Gentle by nature and education, he treated inferiors and equals alike with courtesy. He also upheld men's rights and the law against injustice. This is, no doubt, a flattering portrait. But apart from his involvement in the murder of the atheling Alfred, it would seem the only stain on his character was his greediness for lands.

Cnut's charters have not survived in great quantity, and only one is in favour of Godwin, a grant in 1033 of a nice estate at Polhampton on the river Test in north Hampshire.[3] As Godwin heads the lay witnesses to all Cnut's extant charters after 1023, his seniority would seem to have been uncontested from that point. But little can be said about his activities during the reign. Cnut, whose empire was based on Denmark, also claimed parts of Norway and Sweden, claims that were contested. Although he may have considered England the jewel in the crown, he had to pay close attention to northern affairs and was, indeed, quite often absent from England. He was in Denmark in 1019–20, 1022–3, 1025–6, again in 1026, and in 1026–7. In the spring of 1027 he visited Rome and at Easter attended the coronation of the German king Conrad as Roman emperor.[4]

Godwin accompanied Cnut on one of his northern journeys. A runestone erected to commemorate the death of Bjor Arnsteinson records that Bjor 'found his death in Godwin's host when Cnut sailed to England'.[5] *Vita* implies that Godwin went on one of the earlier visits, perhaps indeed the first. William of Malmesbury, however, perhaps following Chronicle 'E', which records the deaths of many Englishmen apparently in Cnut's defeat by Kings Olaf of Norway and Amund of Sweden at the Holy River in 1025 (?recte 1027), ascribes Godwin's heroic soldiering to that year.[6] But *Vita*'s story seems the more probable: Cnut tested Godwin's character and ability at the earliest opportunity and then gave him his trust. If indeed Godwin remained in England, he was presumably the trusted regent; and the absence of any recorded unrest, although it will have owed something to Cnut's savage destruction of selected magnates at the beginning of the reign, is also a tribute to Godwin's ability.

There were as well two women in Cnut's life who may have had some governmental responsibility during his absences. The king was, seemingly, a bigamist. His first wife was Ælfgifu of Northampton, the daughter of Ealdorman Ælfhelm and Wulfrun. Ælfhelm, a member of a prominent Mercian family, was promoted ealdorman of Northumbria by King Æthelred in 993 and murdered during the 'palace revolution' of 1005–6 at the instigation of Eadric Streona. Two of his sons were then blinded by order of the king.[7] Cnut's second wife was Æthelred's widow, Emma of Normandy, whom he sent for and in July 1017 married. Godwin's relations with these two ladies during Cnut's reign are unknown. But, although Ælfgifu could be considered to be in the Godwin faction (as opposed to that of Eadric Streona), and Emma was the queen Godwin must have served, the earl would seem from later events to have felt no great loyalty to either.

Cnut died on 12 November 1035 at Shaftesbury and was buried in the old minster at Winchester. He was remembered with some respect in the cathedral church. Geoffrey of Cambrai, the prior 1082–1107, devoted to him the first of his historical epigrams. In translation it goes something like this:[8]

Cnut, sprung from the ancient blood of kings,
Had greater power than countless kings.
He girt his noble brow with a triple crown
While he ruled Danes, English and Norwegians.
And he who had been a proud robber, bloodied against the foe,
Held the office of king over those subject to him.
Often leaving the joyous banquets of his own table,
He became a companion of poor monks.
Putting aside pomp, amid a needy crowd,
A fellow slave, he served the slaves of God.
The last light shone for him on the twelfth of November,
And the last day becomes the first day for him.

Cnut was only about forty when he died and, to judge by the consequences, his death had not been expected. He bequeathed a very complicated situation and seven years of disarray. The *Encomium Emmae Reginae*, written shortly after his death, presumably reveals his widow Emma's wishes. Its author claims that Emma made it a precondition of her marriage to Cnut that he would never set up a son by any other wife to rule after him, and that Cnut took an oath to this effect.[9] Such a contract would have been at the expense primarily of Cnut's sons from Ælfgifu of Northampton, Swegen and Harold Harefoot. And it is possible that the one son of Cnut's marriage to Emma, Harthacnut, was designated heir-apparent to all of Cnut's dominions.[10] This would have been Emma's imperious desire. Nevertheless, Cnut's elder son from Ælfgifu, Swegen, had in 1030 with his mother been appointed regent in Norway,[11] and in fact neither thereafter played any discernible part in English history. Swegen died in 1036. The younger brother, Harold Harefoot, however, remained in Mercia, outside Emma's control. Also in the extended family were Emma's sons by King Æthelred, Edward and Alfred, both with potent names; and since the encomiast chose to regard them as full brothers of Harthacnut, he, and presumably Emma, could hardly have excluded them entirely from the list of possible claimants to the throne. But it is clear, both from this and from other evidence, that the queen rated both far below Harthacnut.

In 1035 the eldest of the possible pretenders to the English throne, Edward, was about thirty years old; but none of Cnut's children was much over thirty and Harthacnut was only about eighteen. Moreover, they were all, except one, out of England. Edward and Alfred had been living in Normandy and thereabouts since 1013; Swegen was in Norway, Harthacnut in Denmark; and only Harold Harefoot, apparently a true Mercian, was at hand.

The English magnates met at Oxford, on the frontier between Wessex and Mercia, to discuss the situation.[12] It was a confrontation. According to *The Anglo-Saxon Chronicle* Earl Leofric of Mercia and all the thegns north of the Thames, together with the shipmen of London, chose Harold to rule over the whole of England 'for himself and his brother Harthacnut'. This was clearly envisaged as a stop-gap move, the provision of a ruler without entirely overlooking Harthacnut's claim. But, although there would seem to have been no talk at that juncture of making Harold king, the action had implications for the future, and Earl Godwin, with all the chief men of Wessex, 'opposed it as long as they could'. No doubt Queen Emma rallied them to the cause of Harthacnut; and some men doubted whether Harold was in fact Cnut's or even Ælfgifu's son.[13] He was, however, the only one supported claimant in place; and he sent a force to Winchester, where Emma had taken up residence on her dower lands, to deprive her of such treasures and possessions of her late husband as they could seize, presumably the contents of the royal treasury. But she was allowed to remain at Winchester with Harthacnut's household troops, his housecarls, and, apparently, to hold the whole of Wessex for her absent son. In this fragile situation Godwin's unconditional support was vital.

If Harthacnut had returned immediately, some compromise would probably have been negotiated. But he tarried in Denmark, engaged in a war with Magnus of Norway and clearly giving priority to the defence of the ancestral kingdom. Whereupon Emma turned to her elder sons by Æthelred, Edward and Alfred. It would not seem from the consequences that Godwin supported this policy. It may be that his wife, Gytha, influenced him in favour of the Scandinavian claimants. However that may be, the athelings were not welcomed in England. When in 1036 first Edward, by way of Southampton Water, and then Alfred, by crossing from Wissant or Boulogne, attempted to join their mother, both were attacked. Edward, opposed apparently by local forces, withdrew. Alfred was intercepted by Godwin's troops and taken to Guildford in Surrey, south-west of London. There most of his companions were executed, while he himself was taken to Ely and so carelessly blinded by the king's servants that he died.[14]

Godwin's part in the 'martyrdom' of Alfred was a matter for debate at the time and for long after. It was undeniable that his men had arrested the atheling and, doubtless under the earl's instructions, had surrendered him to Harold's men, and so to his fate. The *Encomium* blames solely Harold, but not by name; Godwin is not mentioned. In Harthacnut's reign Godwin apparently exculpated himself by swearing that he acted only on Harold's orders. If so, he had already by 1036 abandoned Emma and the cause of Harthacnut. This would seem to have been a well-timed and astute manoeuvre, for in 1037 Harold was recognized as king by all men in England, and Emma was expelled, taking refuge at Bruges.[15] There, while waiting for Harthacnut to arrive from Denmark, she had at last an interview with Edward, at which, according to her own story, Edward disclaimed an interest in the English crown and advised her to rely on his half-brother, Harthacnut.[16] He was, indeed, in no position to render her any useful aid at this point; but the affair was probably not as simple as this.

In 1039 Harthacnut made a treaty or truce with Magnus King of Norway and sailed with ten ships for Bruges. Before he advanced further, on 17 March 1040, Harold Harefoot died. Consequently, before midsummer, Harthacnut and Emma sailed for England with sixty ships and received a peaceful welcome at Sandwich. Godwin turned coat once again. Accused by Harthacnut of complicity in Alfred's murder, he gave him a splendid ship, manned by eighty warriors, each magnificently equipped, and took the exculpatory oath already described. He also provided the indispensable support for the new king. On 8 June 1042 Harthacnut himself died at Lambeth, apparently falling dead as he drank at the wedding of Gytha, daughter of the viking Osgot Clapa, to Cnut's Danish factotum, Tovi the Proud.[17] He was succeeded on the throne by his step-brother, Edward the Confessor.

Godwin played a large part in Edward's succession, according to the family's encomiast. He championed the atheling's claim to his ancestral throne so successfully that earls and bishops were sent to fetch him, seemingly from Normandy.[18] Although Godwin's support for Edward at this juncture can hardly be doubted, other sources tell a rather different story.[19] It would seem that Edward returned to England during Harthacnut's short reign, well before his death. The *Encomium Emmae*, in its abrupt closing paragraphs, has Harthacnut, 'gripped by brotherly love', invite Edward to join him and participate in the government. Whereupon mother and sons, united in love, live happily together.[20] According to *The Anglo-Saxon Chronicle*, Edward returned from France to England in 1041, 'was sworn in as king', and remained at court for the rest of Harthacnut's reign. The 'E' version adds that Edward was chosen as Harthacnut's successor by all the people at London before the late king's funeral.[21] The Norman writers, William of Jumièges and William of Poitiers, agree that Harthacnut invited Edward to return because, the latter avers, the king was suffering from a disease and believed he had not long to live. William of Poitiers also takes the opportunity to stress the Norman contribution to Edward's restoration: Harthacnut, the son of the Norman Emma, was doing Edward, a Norman protégé, a good turn. And, many chapters later in his book, he claims boldly that it was by the support and counsel of Duke William that Edward succeeded Harthacnut on the throne.[22]

It is hard to believe that Edward returned uninvited to England. He cannot have forgotten the events of 1036 and his brother Alfred's death. He must have been a little wary of Godwin as well. We can also think that William, still in his uneasy minority, may have seen Edward off with his blessing and perhaps some cash for his expenses. But the prime mover was clearly the ailing and childless Harthacnut. In the circumstances who better than his brother to succeed him? No one mentions the queen mother Emma's active participation; and the general tenor of the *Encomium* is against it. Indeed, there was a rumour that she favoured the candidature of Magnus of Norway.[23] Moreover, Edward's treatment of her immediately after his coronation proves that he believed she had neglected him and his interests. Godwin's own part in this business remains far from clear. But it is unlikely that Harthacnut would have sent for Edward without the earl's concurrence. Godwin might have had some interest in his wife's relation, Swegen Estrithson of Denmark, but could have had none in Magnus. True, it was believed that one of the clauses in the treaty that Harthacnut had made with Magnus in 1039 made each the heir to the other. But there is nothing to suggest that Magnus, who survived until 1047, would have found any support in Wessex or Mercia or much in Northumbria. Edward, as the son of Æthelred the Unready, was the more legitimate claimant.

It would appear, however, that most men, including perhaps Godwin, adhered to him *faute de mieux*. He does not appear to have had much to recommend him in 1042 beyond his lineage. He was landless, unmarried and inexperienced in both war and government. He had, however, outlived all his immediate competitors and had become worldly-wise. For some ten years king and earl were to be yoked uneasily together.

Notes

1. In 1017, according to *ASC, s.a.*, Cnut divided the kingdom into four provinces, reserving Wessex for himself. It is most unlikely that Godwin was made an ealdorman within Eadric Streona's Mercia, Thorkell's East Anglia or Eric's Northumbria. See also ibid. 'E', *s.a.* 1036, and *FNC*, i. 731–3. Cf. above, p. 36, n. 31.
2. *Vita*, pp. 10–11.
3. K., no. 752, S., no. 970. The estate was held by Godwin's son, Earl Tostig, in Edward the Confessor's reign and by William Bertram of the king in 1086. It was rated at $3\frac{1}{2}$ hides and had been worth £12 before 1066. *DB*, i. 47.
4. *FNC*, i. 751–3; Plummer, *Two of the Saxon Chronicles Parallel*, ii. 206–7; Campbell, *Encomium Emmae*, pp. lxii–lxiii; Barlow, 'Two Notes: Cnut's second pilgrimage and Queen Emma's disgrace in 1043', *The Norman Conquest and Beyond* (1983), 50–1.
5. M. Olsen, 'Runestenen ved Oddernes Kirke', *Afhandlinger viede Sophus Bugges Minde* (Christiania, 1908), p. 8.
6. *GR*, i. 220–1. For the proper date, A. Campbell, *Encomium Emmae*, p. 82.
7. Keynes, p. 211.
8. *The Anglo-Latin Satirical Poets and Epigrammatists of the Twelfth Century*, ed. T. Wright (Rolls ser., 1872) ii. 148.
9. *Encomium Emmae*, pp. 32–3.
10. Ibid., pp. 34–5; Körner, p. 55.
11. L.M. Larson, *Cnut the Great* (1912), pp. 248 ff.; M.K. Lawson, *Cnut* (1993), p. 101.
12. *ASC, s.a.*; *FNC*, i. 774–8; Barlow, *Edward*, pp. 42–4.
13. *Encomium Emmae*, p. 40; *ASC*, 'E', *s.a.* 1035.

14. *ASC, s.a.* 1036; Campbell, *Encomium Emmae*, pp. lxiv–lxvii, 41–3; Barlow, *Edward*, pp. 44–6.
15. *ASC, s.a.* 1037.
16. *Encomium Emmae*, pp. 48–9; Barlow, *Edward*, pp. 47, 49–50.
17. John of Worcester, ii. 532–5; *FNC*, i. 789–91; for Tovi, ibid., 792–4.
18. *Vita*, pp. 14–15.
19. Körner, pp. 64–74.
20. *Encomium Emmae*, p. 53.
21. *ASC, s.a.*
22. *GND*, ii. 106–7; *GG*, i, 5, 14, ed. Chibnall, pp. 6–7, 18–21.
23. Barlow, 'Queen Emma's disgrace in 1043', *The Norman Conquest and Beyond*, pp. 51–6.

chapter 3

GODWIN IN POWER,
1042–1051

W ith Edward's succession to the throne in 1042 and his
coronation in 1043, Godwin must have thought he had
once again done well. The Old-English royal dynasty had been
restored after a gap of some 26 years. It was, as *Vita* declares,
the English nation's jubilee.[1] And the displacement of the Danish line had been achieved without much wider disturbance. To
judge by the attestations to royal charters there was massive
continuity in the personnel at court from Cnut's reign into
Edward's, and the names of the royal counsellors had remained
almost exclusively English.[2] Godwin himself exemplifies the stability; and once again he had been the prime mover.

Naturally Godwin exploited the situation to the full. As earl
of Wessex, in which province Edward, at first a virtual stranger,
was bound to live, Godwin's domestic influence was overwhelming; and through his Danish wife Gytha he also had a place in
the Scandinavian world. Swegen king of Denmark, the son of
Estrith, Cnut's sister, was Gytha's nephew; and two of Swegen's
brothers, Earl Beorn and Osbeorn, were living in Wessex.
Swegen's great enemy was Magnus king of Norway; and from
1043 until his death in 1047 it was believed that Magnus was
intending to invade England. In this situation Swegen's resistance to Magnus's attempt to conquer Denmark was Edward's

salvation and something of which Godwin could well have been proud. Moreover, if Swegen harboured any hope of himself sitting on the English throne,[3] he was hardly in those years able to do anything about it.

A new king expected to receive gifts from his subjects and had in return to reward and buy off many nobles and servants. Godwin's encomiast devotes a poem (unfortunately now truncated) to the splendid warship Godwin gave Edward, a vessel seemingly twice the size of the one he had given Harthacnut.

> *A golden lion crowns the stern. A winged*
> *And golden dragon at the prow affrights*
> *The sea, and belches fire with triple tongue.*
> *Patrician purple pranks the hanging sail,*
> *On which are shown th'instructive lineage*
> *And the sea battles of our noble kings.*
> *The yard-arm strong and heavy holds the sails*
> *When wings incarnadine with gold are spread.*[4]

And to Godwin in return went the largest gifts. Almost immediately Edward made Godwin's eldest son, Swegen, an earl, and the second son, Harold, soon followed. Swegen's earldom consisted of two shires subtracted from his father's earldom, Somerset and Berkshire, and three from Mercia, Gloucestershire, Herefordshire and Oxfordshire. Harold received East Anglia. In 1045 Beorn Estrithson, Godwin's Danish nephew and client, was given an earldom in eastern (Danish) Mercia, an appointment which shows that Edward had no fear of an attack from Beorn's brother, King Swegen Estrithson of Denmark.[5] These creations pushed against Leofric of Mercia's territory. Then, on 23 January 1045, the king was also induced to marry Godwin's eldest daughter, Edith. According to *Vita*, she was blessed as wife and crowned as queen. This seems to have been the English custom since the ninth century and a service for the coronation of the queen is included in the 'Edgar' *ordo* of

973.[6] No doubt Godwin and Gytha would have expected a full ceremony. It was Godwin's greatest coup, giving him hope of becoming the grandfather of a king. It was the sort of marriage most of Edward's predecessors had contracted, and merited no comment from the Anglo-Saxon chronicler. It ran its course with no more mishaps than might be expected in a purely political union. It remained, however, childless, and so could be written off in the twelfth century when claims were advanced that Edward had lived a celibate life and was a saint. But there are no good reasons for doubting the reality of the marriage, at least in the early years.

Marriages were normally at that time arranged by the families;[7] and Edward's mother, Emma, as well as Gytha, was presumably involved. In 1043 the groom was approaching 40, the bride was about 22. Edward had for long been a bachelor, a knight errant without an estate, like his younger brother, Alfred; but most princes, however long they postponed marriage — and some did quite recklessly — married in the end if only to produce an heir. The bride was certainly entering matrimony rather older than was usual among the nobility, presumably because Godwin and Gytha had been reserving her for a splendid union. The author of *Vita*, as we have seen, regarded Edith, his patron, as an incomparable bride, virtuous, intelligent, well-educated, talented and generous. She also behaved modestly on informal occasions, often sitting at Edward's feet.[8] Above all, she was a wise counsellor.[9]

Nevertheless, Edith's intrusion into the royal household and court must have been disturbing. Accustomed to the highest Anglo–Danish society, she may have found Edward and his milieu rustic and uncultured. She showed that she was civilized by acquiring a French *femme de chambre*, Matilda, who in due course married a rich English thegn, Ælfweard.[10] And since, according to *Vita*,[11] Edward took little interest in his dress and surroundings, Edith, behaving more like a mother or daughter than a wife, provided him with all the finery she thought appropriate to his majesty. All this, her encomiast believed, the king tolerated with good humour, indeed, would often mention it appreciatively to his courtiers.[12] But it may be that Edith's learning and sophistication were a little intimidating and that Edward found the attention and domestication a bit of a trial. His staff encrusted with gold and gems, his saddle and horse-trappings hung with little golden beasts and birds, the fine Spanish carpets on the floor, the golden embroidered hangings on the throne could have struck him as a silly woman's frippery.

None of this, of course, explains Edith's childlessness, which was obviously unexpected. The author of *Vita* only alludes to it surreptitiously;[13] and it was no doubt a disappointment to all concerned. Both parties came from reasonably fertile families and the union was completely exogamous. If the doctors of the University of Salerno were right in putting the menarche at 12–14 and the menopause at 50, Edith should have been fertile throughout her marriage. They also put men's ability to produce sperm up to sixty, an age at which Edward was approaching death.[14] But it should be noticed that he was, rightly or wrongly, credited with no bastards, something rather unusual at the time.

A visit Edward paid with his wife and mother to Abingdon Abbey, clearly in the early years of the marriage, is described by the house's chronicler.[15] The party had called in to take refreshments and, while touring the buildings, found the monastic children (the oblates) lunching in the refectory. Edith, since she was *urbana*, possibly meaning here a secular woman of fashion, noticed with surprise the early hour of the meal (it was, as usual, an hour before the seniors') and that the boys only had bread to eat. When told that both were usual, she turned to her husband and suggested that, as a consequence of their visit to this 'banquet', he should assign some revenue to the abbey in order to improve the children's diet. Edward received the proposal with good humour and replied with a laugh that he would be only too pleased if someone would give him something with which he could do it. And when Edith answered that she had in fact just acquired a village and would be delighted if Edward would consent to its gift, he agreed that it was a splendid idea. This incident conveys excellently the light-hearted relations between the newly-weds, and also Edith's spontaneous generosity restrained by Edward's thrift.

The first time Godwin is found in attendance on the new king is immediately after the coronation, which he would have attended, when Edward led the three greatest earls, Leofric of Mercia, Godwin and the Dane, Siward of Northumbria (the chronicler puts them in that order) in an attack on his mother at Winchester in order to despoil her of the royal treasury and all her wealth. He was not only looking to his own enrichment but also punishing her for her long neglect of his interests.[16] It was rumoured that Emma favoured Magnus of Norway as Harthacnut's successor.[17] That Edward repeated Harold Hare-foot's raid on Emma in similar circumstances, suggests that the queen mother remained greedy for wealth and influence. She was, however, soon pardoned by her last surviving son. After his marriage it seems she ceased to witness his charters, pushed into the background perhaps by convention, the queen's hos-tility, or both. In 1044 and 1045 Edward commanded a fleet at Sandwich in case Magnus invaded,[18] and it can be assumed that Godwin was there with his ships and some of his sons.

For Godwin to retain a dominant position, it was necessary for him to establish a personal rapport with Edward like that he had enjoyed with Cnut. But it was not to be. They spoke different languages; Edward had deep-seated grievances; and there could have been no mutual attraction. The king evidently soon resented the earl's power and patronage. At first he could do little to curb them. He had returned to England from his long exile with no great company, of which but a few can be identified — mostly clerks, for it was these whom he first tried to reward in the kingdom.[19] He could also play off the other two great earls against the earl of Wessex. Leofric of Mercia, scion of a long-established dynasty, was probably beginning to feel the threat of encirclement from the Godwins. Siward of Northumbria's ambition seems to have been to expand north into Scotland; but he would most likely follow Leofric's lead. And in 1045 occurred the first of the splits in Godwin's family. An important theme in *Vita* is the necessity of harmony for the family's wellbeing. The author likens Godwin's sons to four rivers out of paradise.

> *O happy world if each would keep its course*
> *And water its own lands, with pacts observed,*
> *As the celestial order has ordained!*
> . . .   .
> *But if malignant envy breaks this pact*
> *By revolution, O what ruin comes!*[20]

The first to break the pact, a man whom the encomiast never names but may allude to in that poem, was the eldest son, Swegn. This wild man, who, as we have noticed, claimed that his real father was Cnut,[21] from the start went his own turbulent way. The inclusion of Herefordshire and Gloucestershire in his earldom involved him in the complex politics of the Welsh march, in which the earl of Mercia was the prime English mover. In 1046 Swegn went with Gruffydd ap Llywelyn, king of Gwynedd and Powis in North Wales, and as such a rival of Leofric's, on an expedition into South Wales.[22] That might well have been considered aid for an enemy of the English. And to crown his defiance, on his way back 'he ordered the abbess of Leominster to be brought to him, and he kept her as long as it suited him, and then let her go home.' Whether this was seduction or rape of Eadgifu, who could have been a kinswoman, is not known. But, according to Worcester tradition, Swegn kept her as a wife for a whole year until the threats of Archbishop Eadsige of Canterbury and Lyfing bishop of Worcester caused him to give her up. In revenge Swegn and his friends deprived the church of Worcester of Maesbrook, Hopton and North Cleobury and many other places in Shropshire.[23] The king, no doubt, at the instigation of the church, outlawed him but, to avoid further hurting the family, divided all, or part, of his earldom between his brother Harold and his cousin Beorn. Swegen wintered at Bruges in Flanders before going on to Denmark and involving himself in the Scandinavian war, presumably on the side of his namesake cousin, King Swegn Estrithson,[24] although, according to Anglo-Saxon Chronicle 'D', he committed crimes against the Danes. King Swegen in 1047 appealed to Edward for help, and Godwin advised sending 50 ships; but Earl Leofric led the opposition to this; and Godwin, perhaps for the first time and certainly not the last, was overruled.[25] From 1046 until 1060 the queen witnesses none of Edward's extant charters. Magnus's death on 25 October 1047 allowed Swegen Estrithson to recover control of Denmark and that famous viking adventurer, Harold Sigurdsson (Hardrada), Magnus's paternal uncle, to take over Norway. Harold married Elisev, daughter of Yaroslav the Wise, Grand Prince of Kiev; and after Harold's death at Stamfordbridge in 1066, Elislev married Swegn Estrithson.

The revolutions led to renewed viking activity in the North Sea. In 1048 two pirates, Lothen and Yrling, attacked Sandwich, Thanet and Essex and sold their plunder in Flanders. In 1049 the Emperor Henry III, tired of Baldwin of Flanders' participation in the Lotharingian rebellion, asked Swegen of Denmark and Edward for help, and Edward summoned a large fleet to Sandwich.[26] In the summer Earl Swegen, with seven or eight ships, sailed past Sandwich and put into Bosham harbour in Sussex, a family estate. He then travelled overland to seek the king's pardon and the recovery of his lands. He seems to have rested his hopes on his Danish cousin, Earl Beorn. But his brother, Harold, was implacably opposed, and Beorn may have wavered. Godwin's position is unknown. In the end Edward ordered Swegen out of the country and gave him four days in which to rejoin his ships.

It so happened at this time that an Irish viking fleet, in alliance with Gruffydd ap Rhydderch, king of South Wales, was raiding up the River Severn; and Edward dispatched from Sandwich two royal vessels and the Wessex squadron of forty-two ships under Godwin, Beorn and Tostig, to deal with this menace and probably also to keep an eye on Swegen.[27] While the English fleet lay weatherbound at Pevensey, Swegen reappeared and once again appealed for help with the king. This time Beorn agreed and joined his cousin with just three men. Swegen took him to his ships at Bosham where he had him seized and carried on board. His ships then sailed west, and at Dartmouth Beorn was murdered and buried on shore, either as punishment for failing to support his cousin at Sandwich or as a result of a further quarrel. Later, Harold gave his cousin a splendid burial at Winchester in the presence of a large company of his friends and the sailors from London, probably the company which he may have commanded. He was laid to rest in the Old Minster, with his uncle King Cnut. Then the king and the whole army declared Swegen *nithing*, a wicked man and outlaw. After the murder six of Swegen's ships had deserted, and Swegen sailed with the two remaining to Bruges where he was welcomed by Count Baldwin.

It would seem from this episode and from his exclusion from *Vita* that Swegen regarded himself as a Dane (like his mother) and perhaps as no real member of the Godwin family. In return he was shunned by his brothers and his sister the queen. Only his Danish cousin Beorn made some gesture of support, and got little thanks. His father seems to have tried to avoid getting involved. The family in fact, except for the loss of Beorn, came out in some ways strengthened; and in the following year, 1050, Bishop Ealdred of Worcester, who knew Earl Swegen well, while returning from Rome met him in Flanders, presumably accepted his repentance for having debauched an abbess, brought him back to England and obtained for him the royal pardon.[28] It would seem from subsequent events that Swegen recovered some of his lands in the south west and, since he witnessed a royal charter in 1050, his comital title as well. But he was not happy with the French colony and castles that the king's nephew, Ralf of Mantes, had established in Herefordshire, although other members of the family seem usually to have been on friendly terms with Ralf, who married a woman named Gytha and called a son Harold.[29] How willingly Edward accepted Swegen's return and at least partial reinstatement cannot be said. But it is possible that he hoped it might upset his wife's family.

By 1050 the king had recovered very well from his weak start and had become so confident that he was prepared to quarrel with the Godwins. What may have liberated him was the unfruitfulness of his five-year-old marriage. Even if he was not greatly concerned over who would reign after him, the situation gave him diplomatic leverage. He might be interested in a more fertile partner and he could investigate and raise the hopes of his relatives on the Continent. There is no doubt that several foreign princes did become increasingly interested in the succession. There were those who claimed through Cnut, such as Swegen of Denmark and, more remotely, the Norwegians; there was William of Normandy, through Edward's mother his cousin-once-removed; and there were Edward's own kinsmen, descendants of Æthelred the Unready, scattered across Europe, such as Edmund Ironside's descendants in Hungary, Godgifu's children by Drogo count of Mantes, Count Walter III and Ralf earl of Hereford, as well as Godgifu's second husband, Eustace

II count of Boulogne. At the same time, although Edith's childlessness was a blow to the Godwins, it did not destroy their diplomatic importance, for while they controlled the southern half of the kingdom, Godwin had still to be regarded as a potential king-maker. No foreign pretender could make much headway without coming to terms with him and his family.

It is against this diplomatic background that Godwin's fall in 1051 must be viewed.[30] The basic cause was Edward's desire to get the Godwins off his back. The immediate causes were accidental. Godwin, somewhat unusually for him, got involved in a dispute over a church appointment. When Eadsige, archbishop of Canterbury, died on 29 October 1050, the monks of Christ Church elected one of their own number, Æthelric, a relation of Godwin's, and called on the earl to support them. Free elections were not usual at the time and, not surprisingly, the king disregarded the monks' wishes and Godwin's advocacy and nominated his friend, Robert of Jumièges, a Norman monk, bishop of London since 1046. Robert would seem to have been an entirely suitable candidate. Canterbury, however, was in Godwin's earldom, Æthelric was a kinsman, and the earl clearly was offended. Nor can it be thought that Æthelric was completely unworthy. He may well be the second of that name to become Bishop of Selsey in 1058, only to be deposed on unknown grounds by Archbishop Lanfranc in 1070, despite the strong misgivings of Pope Alexander II.

The author of *Vita* puts the whole blame for Edward's proscription of the Godwins in 1051 on Robert of Jumièges. The new archbishop of Canterbury complained to the king, on this matter with justice, that Godwin had despoiled Canterbury of some estates, reminded him that the earl had been responsible for his brother Alfred's death in 1036 and, moreover, alleged that now he was planning likewise to kill Edward. It was the king's putting Godwin on trial for these misdeeds that led to the earl's downfall. This must have been Edith's story. But it is not the story told by *The Anglo-Saxon Chronicle*, which may be a contemporary witness here. According to this source, which completely ignores Robert's part, it was the visit of Eustace of Boulogne to his brother-in-law, the king, in the autumn of 1051 which sparked off the quarrel. The purpose of the visit is not stated – 'Eustace told the king what he wished and then went homewards'. What these evasive words conceal is uncertain. It would seem that the count was no friend of Godwin's, and it could be that he came to tell Edward that it was about time he got himself a new wife and should look to Eustace's family or connections for an heir. It is unlikely that he was an emissary of Baldwin of Flanders or William of Normandy.

However that may be, on the return journey Eustace and his men had a meal at Canterbury and then pushed on to Dover to seek billets for the night. Possibly because they had had trouble there on their inward journey or because they foresaw trouble from Godwin's officials, on approaching Dover they put on their coats of mail and indeed were soon in conflict with the householders. After a reluctant and wounded landlord killed one of Eustace's men, these went on the rampage and in the fighting more than 20 of the townsfolk were killed; and Eustace's losses were nineteen killed and many more wounded. Eustace returned with his shrunken retinue to Edward and complained. The king ordered Godwin to go and punish Kent and Dover for this outrage; and when the earl refused, Edward summoned all the magnates to a council to be held at Gloucester on or about 8 September 1051. Godwin and his two eldest sons, Swegen and Harold, each with his men, came together at their manor of Beverstone, some 15 miles south of Gloucester and 10 miles from the junction of the Fosse Way, Ermine Street and Icknield Way, intending to go to the council. Earls Leofric, Siward and Ralf, at Edward's behest, joined the king with their armed forces. And it looked like war. However, those with the king decided that all involved should give hostages to him and meet again in London on 21 September when the charges against Godwin would be heard. The aim was to allow tempers to cool and avoid a fight.

Godwin had been out-manoeuvred, and discovered not only that the king was implacable but also that he and his family were for the moment friendless. All his demands for a lawful trial in which he could prove his innocence, presumably by oath, possibly with the aid of helpers, were refused, as were also his requests for safe-conducts and hostages to allow him to attend the council in safety. As he and his sons made their way south of the Thames towards London, while the king and his friends travelled by the more northerly route, they suffered some desertions. When they arrived at their manor of South-wark, at the Surrey end of the old London bridge, they were required to transfer all their thegns to the king's service. Godwin and Harold complied; and either now or earlier, Swegen was outlawed out of hand. Bishop Stigand of Winchester was the intermediary between the royalists and the Godwins. *Vita*, per-haps imaginatively, claims that Edward dispatched Stigand to Godwin with this 'insoluble' medial judgement: 'That he could hope for the king's peace only when he gave him back his brother alive with all his men and all their possessions which had been taken from them when alive and when dead.' On delivering these grimly jesting words, Stigand wept, and Godwin pushed away the table in front of him, mounted horse and fled. They had lost the means of fighting. To escape was their only hope.

The chapter devoted in *Vita* to this disaster is preceded by an enigmatic poem in which it is foreseen and explained.[31] It was caused by the breaking of pacts by Godwin's four sons. These delinquents are not named, but are presumably those sons whom the author names elsewhere, Harold, Tostig, Gyrth and Leofwine. But as he intrudes Edith, and names her, into the poem — she is the peace-lover and peace-provider — it is just possible that the destroyer of peace is Swegen. This could have been Edith's view of his disruptive behaviour. But what pacts the children of Godwin made, and broke, it is impossible to say. Certainly the family split up in October 1051; but, except for Swegen, it reunited harmoniously in 1052. Godwin made for Bosham, his harbour on the Sussex coast and, according to Chronicle 'D', was accompanied, or joined there, by his wife Gytha, and his sons, Swegen, Tostig, with his wife Judith of Flanders, and Gyrth. They loaded a ship which had been prepared for them with all the money and treasure it could carry and, in one or more ships, sailed for Flanders and the protection of Count Baldwin. Godwin's alliance with Flanders, which was of importance to the family in 1065 and later years, shows that there were limits to his Danishness. Harold and Leofwine, however, went to Bristol in Swegen's earldom, where Swegen had a ship ready to sail; and they crossed with great difficulty because of stormy weather to Ireland, where they spent the winter under the protection of King Diarmait mac Máel na mBó, lord of Leinster and Dublin. Swegen may well have originally intended joining the Scandinavian colony of Dublin under its king, Eachmargach.[32]

When the Godwins fled instead of standing trial, Edward took measures against them. He sent Bishop Ealdred of Worcester from London with an armed force in pursuit of Harold; 'but they could not — or would not — intercept him'. All the fugitives were outlawed and their earldoms and lands forfeited. Some of the remainder of Swegen's earldom in the South-West was granted to Odda of Deerhurst, said by William of Malmesbury to be a kinsman of Edward; and Harold's earldom of East Anglia went to Ælfgar, Earl Leofric's son. The bulk of Godwin's earldom of Wessex Edward probably kept in his own hands. The queen, whom Archbishop Robert urged the king to divorce, was sent to a nunnery, either Wherwell in Hampshire, where Edward's (? half-) sister was abbess, or Wilton, where she had been educated, or perhaps the one before the other. She was also despoiled of all her lands and movables. One version of the Chronicle (D) adds: 'Then forthwith Count William came from overseas with a great force of Frenchmen, and the king received him and as many of his companions as suited him, and let him go again.' This is no confusion with Count Eustace's visit, which the chronicler had already described; but it is strange that both the Abingdon and Canterbury versions, whose compilers were well placed to report such an incursion, ignore it. It cannot have been in the common source, the 'X' chronicle. It would, however, help to explain how hostages given by the Godwins, perhaps at this time, passed into William's hands.

The author of *Vita* inserts at this point a poem on Godwin's downfall.[33] This innocent man, a spring of pure water, as the poet had said earlier, was defiled by blame for a crime he had not committed. Often enough the more faithful a man is proved, the greater the punishment he is awarded, for example the Bible characters Susanna, the boy Joseph, and Jesus Christ. A thousand cases could be cited from the past and the present. *Vita* also contributes the information that all these things happened at the very time when 'Earl' Tostig was celebrating his nuptials with Judith, Baldwin V's sister and Edward's niece. Tostig certainly married Judith, who was the daughter of Count Baldwin IV of Flanders and his second wife, Eleanor of Normandy, and so Baldwin V's half-sister and Edward's cousin-once-removed; and the marriage to cement the alliance between the Godwins and the count as likely as not took place at this time. But it does not seem that Tostig was an earl in 1051 or, *pace* Chronicle 'D', likely that Judith was in England.

The family had obviously made contingency plans for an armed return before they split up in October 1051. Pirate vessels and crews could be enlisted at Bruges and Dublin and both parties had taken plenty of money. They knew that Edward would see to the English defences; but they were also aware that viking raids could rarely be intercepted and prevented. It was just as necessary to recruit sympathisers and allies in the kingdom. And here the king would seem to have played into the outlaws' hands. By his ruthless elimination of all the Godwins and by supporting a Norman clique of courtiers and church-men, and perhaps by welcoming and encouraging the duke himself, he aroused sympathy for the victims and anxiety over the implications of the revolution. Moreover, the Godwins were spared one embarrassment. Swegen had decided — perhaps it had determined his decision not to go to Dublin — to atone for his sins by a pilgrimage to Jerusalem. Adven-turous to the end, he is said to have walked barefoot from Bruges to the holy city. On 29 September 1052 he died of cold at or near Constantinople on the return journey. William of Malmesbury improved on this by having him killed by Saracens.[34] His meritorious end must have come as a relief to everyone. His one known child, Hacon, was in the hands of William of Normandy.

Vita, always anxious to emphasize Godwin's preference for peace, claims that from Bruges the earl petitioned the king for mercy and permission to appear before him and lawfully prove his innocence of any crime, and that both Baldwin of Flanders and Henry I of France urged Edward to permit it.[35] But when these overtures were rebuffed, Godwin assembled a fleet in the River Yser, at Nieuport, between Ostend and Dunkerque. The family clearly intended to return to England, if necessary by force; but they could not have expected to defeat the king if he was fully supported by Earls Leofric and Siward, even though he had in 1051 paid off the last of the foreign crews. The Godwins must have set their hopes on rallying the thegns of their old earldoms and obtaining at least the neutrality of Earls Leofric and Siward. They had to make a show of force while waving olive branches. Godwin persevered in this vein until the end. Harold, however, probably then in his mid twenties, was not so conciliatory.

Edward was kept on the alert in 1052. First Llywelyn ap Gruffydd, king of Gwynedd and Powys, ravaged Herefordshire, probably exploiting the general insecurity rather than striking a blow on behalf of his old ally, Earl Swegen. On 14 March Edward's mother, Emma of Normandy, died after an eventful life, and was buried by her son not with his father, Æthelred, at St Paul's, London, but at Winchester with her second husband, King Cnut. For Edward it may have signified the snapping of one more shackle. About this time his 'portrait' on the silver pennies was turned to face right and, instead of a debased classical image, appeared the head and shoulders of a bearded warrior wearing a conical helmet and holding a sceptre before his face.[36] It was an unusually virile design. To meet the danger of invasion from the Godwins, Edward put Somerset and Devon on a war footing against Harold, and against Godwin stationed a fleet at Sandwich, some forty small vessels under Earls Ralf and Odda, two who had benefited from the Godwins' disgrace.

Godwin was the first to move, sailing from the Yser on 22 June. He passed Sandwich unchallenged and landed at Dungeness, the point in south-west Kent where the coastline turns decisively west. He is said to have had a warm welcome. When the royal fleet went in pursuit Godwin sailed on westerly to Pevensey Bay in Sussex. But there was no sign of Harold; and a great storm blew both squadrons back up the Channel, Godwin returning to Bruges, the royal ships to Sandwich and then up the Thames to London, where amid much confusion the fleet was partially decommissioned. The main profit to Godwin from this expedition was the knowledge that he would be welcomed back in Wessex.

Harold and Leofwine with nine ships eventually crossed from Dublin into the Bristol Channel and ravaged for provisions on the boundary of Somerset and Devon. At Porlock they routed the local forces sent against them, killing more than thirty 'good thegns' as well as other men; and then sailed round Lands End and up the English Channel. *Vita* even alleges that they continued ravaging the coastal areas until they met up with their father. Meanwhile Godwin had sailed again from the Yser to the Isle of Wight, which he ravaged, then westwards to Portland in Dorset where, probably late in August, at last he met his sons. *Vita* relates ecstatically:

> With great joy the father and brothers looked on each other again and marvelled at each other's labours and dangers, now at an end. The sea was covered with ships. The sky glittered with the press of weapons. And so at length, with the soldiers made more resolute by mutual exhortation, they crossed the Kentish sea, as it is called, and with the ships astern in long line, entered the mouth of the River Thames.[37]

From Wight onwards, however, the outlaws changed their tactics. According to the Chronicle, they merely required provisions from the coastal areas, and encouraged well-wishers to join them. Especially they recruited all the sailors they could. They took ships and hostages from Romney, Hythe, Folkestone, Dover and Sandwich; and in the end assembled quite a formidable fleet. It would seem that in the south-east of the kingdom both the popularity of the Godwins and a dislike of the king's French friends were strongly felt. Godwin's armada rounded the North Foreland and, while most of the ships sailed round Sheppey to the Thames, some penetrated south of the island into the Medway, on the way doing much damage and burning Milton Regis to the ground. Perhaps these were Harold's ships.

Meanwhile the king, fully alerted to the danger, decided to make a stand at London, according to *Encomium Emmae*, 'a most populous place'.[38] He had some fifty ships, under Earls

Odda and Ralf, on the Thames, stationed upstream from London Bridge, a structure which could serve as a great barrier to
a hostile navy. Edward also summoned all who owed him military service to appear at London with their troops. But these,
the chronicle states, came in slowly. Godwin too had appealed
for military help from his friends; and the resulting land force
approached London from the west and on the north bank of
the river. On 14 September Godwin's fleet reached Southwark,
once his own manor, where he negotiated with the Londoners
and was awarded safe passage on the tide through London
Bridge while hugging the south bank. As a result the royal
squadron was threatened from both sides: the Godwinist land
army on the Middlesex bank and Godwin's fleet across the
river. From this threatening position Godwin tried to negotiate.

Through emissaries the earl asked the king for the restoration of all the family's earldoms and everything else that had
been taken from them. Edward wanted to fight; and there were
belligerents also on Godwin's side; but the general wish was for
reconciliation. The unwillingness of Earls Leofric and Siward to
fight the Godwins was decisive. Bishop Stigand seems again to
have been the leading intermediary; and when it was agreed
that both sides should give hostages, Edward's support began
to collapse. The Norman prelates, Robert of Canterbury, Ulf
of Dorchester and William of London, together with some
foreign soldiers, fled from the city. Robert went to live, until
his death in 1055, in his old monastery of Jumièges and no
doubt influenced the chronicle which William of Jumièges was
then writing. In England Edward, after the flight of his foreign
friends, ordered a great council to meet outside London — at
his palace at Westminster according to *Vita*;[39] and it was attended by all the great earls and the chief men of the kingdom.
Godwin and Harold appeared fully armed as for battle and
were met by Edward at the entrance to his palace. Whereupon
Godwin cast aside his weapons, threw himself at Edward's feet

and made once again his standard plea. Let the king allow him to purge himself of all the crimes of which he stood accused and, when proved innocent, grant him his peace.

Edward, clearly unwillingly but constrained by lack of support and the threat of violence from the Godwins, returned them their weapons and conducted them into the palace. There, after Godwin had expounded his case and declared that he and his sons were innocent of all the charges that had been brought against them, the king, on the advice of his wise men, the *witan*, gave Godwin the kiss of peace, forgave all wrongs and granted his full favour to him and all his sons, together with the restoration of their earldoms and former possessions. This amnesty was extended to all the men with Godwin. The queen was sent for and ceremoniously restored to the king's bed-chamber and all her possessions. On the other hand, Archbishop Robert together with many other Frenchmen — those who had promoted injustice, pronounced unjust judgements and given bad counsel — were outlawed. But there were exceptions: those foreigners whom the king wanted to keep with him and were loyal to him and all the people. Bishop William was soon welcomed back to London. But Robert remained abroad and was replaced at Canterbury by Bishop Stigand of Winchester, who for the rest of the reign held these two sees in plurality.

A poem in *Vita* is devoted to Godwin's restoration.[40] He is likened to the Biblical David, who became King Saul's son-in-law, vice-regent and a victorious general against the Philistines, only to incur the king's murderous jealousy. Yet, although David had several opportunities to kill Saul, he 'abhorred the sin of regicide', would not attack 'the Lord's anointed', and always spared him. There may be a sub-text that Godwin, if not like David his persecutor's successor on the throne, would nevertheless through his descendants establish a new royal dynasty.

The alleged visit of Duke William of Normandy to Edward's court immediately after the dispossession of the Godwins in 1051 introduces, however, a competitor. William's claim to succeed Edward is developed at length in Archdeacon William of Poitiers's panegyric of the duke written before 1077. And one of the first planks in the case is Edward's nomination of William as his heir with the assent of the English magnates.[41] In the context of the diplomatic exchanges between King Harold and the Norman invader immediately before the battle of Hastings, the duke is made to claim that Edward had nominated him as his heir in gratitude for the hospitality he had received during his enforced stay in the duchy (1016–1041), and that Edward's nomination had been supported by the English magnates. Archbishop Stigand and Earls Godwin, Leofric and Siward had taken corporeal oaths that they would do nothing to harm his cause and would accept him as their lord after Edward's death. Moreover, Edward had given him as hostages Godwin's son and *nepos*, grandson or nephew. All this had been done in William's absence.

If Stigand's title of archbishop is correct, the event has to be dated after September 1052, when he took over Canterbury, and before Easter 1053, when Godwin died. Such a date would seem unlikely. The Godwins were then back in power, and the adoption of William as Edward's son could have been regarded by Godwin as an insult to his daughter. If, however, the title is a mistake, a date before September 1051 is possible, and Godwin's enforced agreement to the plan could have been a further cause of his quarrel with the king. But this oath, like that of Harold in 1064–5, which is the next plank in the Norman case and is associated with the other in William of Poitiers's exposition of it, is just as difficult to pin down.

There is also the problem of the hostages. The son of Godwin is undoubtedly Wulfnoth whose fate is well documented. As nothing is known of Godwin's nephews, a grandson has usually been preferred, and in particular Hacon, a son of Earl Swegen. These could have been taken to Normandy by Archbishop Robert of Canterbury on his way to Rome for the conferment of his pallium in the autumn of 1050 or the spring of 1051 when, according to William of Poitiers, he conveyed Edward's promise of the throne to William. Alternatively, they could have been given as hostages to Edward later in 1051 and transferred to William when he visited England in the autumn. They were presumably out of the kingdom before the Godwins' return in 1052 or they would have secured their release. E.A. Freeman disbelieved in the bequest, the oaths, and the sending of hostages at this time: the Norman case was an absurd fabrication.[42] But the improbability should not be exaggerated. Childlessness was an enormous diplomatic asset which, it seems, Edward knew how to exploit to the full. Several princes claimed that he had dangled the prospect of the succession before their eyes. In 1051 he was still in his forties and would appear to have been in excellent health. He was in fact to live for another fifteen years.

Godwin, however, did not do so well. It was just when the English political scene was settling down again after this turbulent interval that he, seemingly unexpectedly, died. Together with his sons, Harold, Tostig and Gyrth, he spent Easter 1053 with the king at Winchester. On Easter Monday, 12 April, when they were dining with Edward, Godwin collapsed speechless, presumably suffering a stroke, and was carried by his sons into the royal bedchamber. He died on the following Thursday, 15 April, without having recovered his senses, and was buried in the Old Minster with his first great patron, King Cnut.[43] If he was indeed just about sixty, the exertions and excitements of the years 1051-2 may have been too much for him. *Vita* claims that the earl had made many gifts of ornaments and lands to the Minster for the redemption of his soul. But only gifts of Gytha for this purpose have survived in the records. However, Godwin is listed last of the ducal benefactors of the New Minster (Hyde) at Winchester.[44] And there is no reason to doubt *Vita*'s belief that Godwin was greatly honoured by the people. He had been their and the kingdom's *nutricius*, a guardian, tutor and father. He had also lived long enough to salvage the family's fortunes. He had helped to steer the kingdom through perilous years made even more difficult by some short reigns and much erratic government. And he had also held his family together despite Swegen's irresponsible behaviour. No doubt his wife, Gytha, with her links with the Danish aristocracy and conspicuous loyalty to her husband, had also played a part. And his daughter, Queen Edith, although unable always to control her husband, is said by *Vita* always to have advised him well.

Notes

1. *Vita*, pp. 14–15.
2. Barlow, *Edward*, p. 75.
3. Ibid, pp. 92–3.
4. *Vita*, pp. 20–1, translated Barlow.
5. *FNC*, ii, app. G, 'The great earldoms under Edward', pp. 571–85, map p. 584; Barlow, *Edward*, map p. 356.
6. *Vita*, pp. 24–5; Barlow, *Edward*, pp. 65, 80–5. OV, however, in an interpolation into *GND*, claims that the alliance with Godwin and the marriage was on the advice of the Normans: *GND*, ii, 108–9.
7. Barlow, *The Feudal Kingdom of England, 1042–1216*, 5th edn (1999), London, Longman, pp. 213–14.
8. Above, pp. 33–4.
9. *Vita*, pp. 6–7, 26–7, 80–1.
10. *Hemingi Chartularium*, ed. T. Hearne (Oxford, 1723), i, 253.
11. *Vita*, pp. 22–5.
12. Ibid, pp. 64–5, cf. 122–3.
13. He refers to the zeal with which she reared, educated, adorned and showered with motherly love those boys who were said to be of royal stock: *Vita*, pp. 24–5.

14. *The Prose Salernitan Questions*, ed. B. Lawn (1979), pp. 196, 233–4; 92, cf. 6.
15. *The Abingdon Chronicle*, i, 459–61.
16. *ASC*, 'C', 'D'.
17. Barlow, 'Queen Emma's disgrace in 1043', *The Norman Conquest and Beyond*, pp. 51–6. According to *King Harald's Saga*, cap. 79, Tostig in 1066 told King Harald of Norway that Magnus had not tried to conquer England because all the people there wanted Edward as their king.
18. *ASC*, 'C', 'D'.
19. *Vita*, pp. 28–9; Barlow, *Edward*, pp. 50–3.
20. *Vita*, pp. 26–7.
21. See above, p. 33.
22. *ASC*, 'C'; K.L. Maund, 'The Welsh alliances of Earl Ælfgar of Mercia', *ANS*, xi (1989), 183–4.
23. *ASC*, 'C'; *Hemingi Chartularium ecclesiae Wigorniensis*, i. 275–6; A. Williams, 'The spoliation of Worcester', *ANS*, xix (1997), 385–6. Cf. the story of how Godwin obtained Berkeley Abbey, above, p. 32.
24. *ASC*, 'E'.
25. *ASC*, 'D'; John of Worcester, ii. 544–5.
26. *ASC*, 'C', 'D', 'E', for this and the following. Barlow, *Edward*, pp. 98–101.
27. *ASC*, 'D'; John of Worcester, ii. 548–51.
28. *ASC*, 'C', 'E'; John of Worcester, ii. 550–1.
29. Barlow, *Edward*, p. 103, n. 2.
30. *ASC, s.a.*; John of Worcester, ii. 558–63; *Vita*, pp. 28–39; Barlow, *Edward*, pp. 106–17.
31. *Vita*, pp. 26–9.
32. Seán Duffy, 'Ireland's Hastings: the Anglo-Norman Conquest of Dublin', *ANS*, xx (1998), 69–85, at 76–7.
33. *Vita*, pp. 38–9.
34. *GR*, i. 245.
35. For this and the following, *Vita*, pp. 38–47; *ASC, s.a.*; John of Worcester, ii. 566–71; Barlow, *Edward*, pp. 118–34.
36. G.C. Brooke, *English Coins* (1932), type 6, pl. xvii, no. 10; Barlow, *Edward*, pl. 10.
37. *Vita*, pp. 42–3.
38. *Encomium Emmae*, p. 23.

39. *Vita*, pp. 44–5.
40. Ibid., pp. 44–7.
41. *GG*, ii, 12, ed. Chibnall, pp. 120–1. R. Foreville, 'Aux origines de la renaissance juridique et influences romanisantes chez Guillaume de Poitiers, biographe du Conquérant', *Moyen Age*, lviii (1952), 43–83, at pp. 61–76.
42. *FNC*, ii, app. note U.
43. *ASC, s.a.*; *Vita*, pp. 46–9.
44. *Liber Vitae: Register and Martyrology of New Minster and Hyde Abbey, Winchester*, ed. W. de Gray Birch, Hampshire Record Soc. (1982), p. 22.

chapter 4

GODWIN'S CHILDREN, 1053–1062

❦

On Godwin's death the king appointed the earl's eldest surviving son, Harold, to succeed his father in the earldom of Wessex. In Scandinavia, where it was believed that Harold was junior to Tostig, it was thought that he had been brought up at Edward's court as his foster-son, as the king had no children of his own (*King Harald's Saga*, cap. 75). It was also thought that, whereas Tostig was made commander of the English army, Harold was put in charge of the royal exchequer (cap. 77). *Vita*, rather better informed in connection with Harold's succession to Wessex, calls him at pages 46–7 the wisest of the brothers and claims that at his promotion the whole country rejoiced. To East Anglia, which Harold relinquished, Edward appointed Ælfgar, Earl Leofric of Mercia's son. The effect was to strengthen the Mercian family at the expense of the Godwins. Each now had control over a latitudinal stretch of the kingdom, with the third, the northern tranche, still in the hands of Earl Siward the Dane. In the Welsh march Earl Ralf of Mantes had, it seems, been left undisturbed in 1052; and Earl Odda of Deerhurst appears to have remained in control of some other border shires. This was a compromise situation at the expense of Tostig, Godwin's second surviving son, now married to Judith of Flanders and waiting impatiently for an earldom. It was also a sign that all parties were, for the moment, prepared to tolerate the others. But Tostig may have acquired a grievance. It could be — it is even likely — that he and Harold were always rivals, the cadet resenting his senior's advantages. But the story of how, when boys, they had a fight at Edward's court and the king prophesied the events of 1065–6, does not appear before Ailred of Rievaulx's *Vita Sancti Edwardi*, written in 1163.[1]

Edward had been humiliated; but he had learnt the lesson that he could not rely on a 'king's party' and was powerless without the cooperation of some of the great provincial earls. He had, however, probably acknowledged William of Normandy's interest in the succession and by 1065 the duke had Godwin's youngest son, Wulfnoth, and the late Earl Swegen's son, Hacon, in his custody.[2] Although it is not clear exactly when and how these got into his hands, the likeliest scenario is that Godwin surrendered them to Edward some time in the autumn of 1051, and that the king transferred them to William when the duke visited him later in that year. If Edward had indeed made William his heir, the transfer of Godwin's hostages would have been to bind that family to the scheme. But it could also have been a spiteful gesture which gave Edward himself some control over the family's behaviour.

The events of 1051–2 must have affected, presumably adversely, the relations between the king and the queen. It would appear that Edith began increasingly to look to the advancement of her brothers, and, as active support for the king declined, to become a woman of importance, even perhaps embittered and unpleasant. An anecdote in Hariulf's Chronicle of Saint-Riquier, a distinguished monastery in Ponthieu, a county in the extreme north-west of France, is suggestive.[3] Hariulf claimed that Abbot Gervin I often visited England, where the abbey had estates, and was a friend of the queen. But once when Edith welcomed him at court with a kiss of greeting and peace, Gervin withdrew his face in horror; and the queen, furious at being snubbed by a monk, withheld the gifts she had made him. However, after Edward had reproved her and courtiers had intervened, she understood the abbot's scruples, repented of her anger and gave him an amice (a square or oblong cloth with strings attached worn round the neck by a priest when celebrating mass), ornamented with orphrey and precious stones, a vestment so splendid that it was coveted and eventually acquired by Gervin's bishop, Guy of Amiens, the author of the famous poem on the battle of Hastings. Moreover, Edith was converted to the abbot's view, and ordered her own abbots and bishops in future to refuse the kisses of women. Edith was a wilful and increasingly powerful woman.[4]

For twelve years after Godwin's death in 1053 the family prospered. Much of its success was due to Harold's qualities and wise behaviour. He seems in the beginning to have been on good terms with his sister, the queen, and to have achieved at least a working relationship with his brother-in-law, Edward. Indeed, he acted increasingly as the king's lieutenant. Those two military earls, Ralf of Mantes and Odda of Deerhurst, remained on the Welsh border. Harold got on well with the former and seems to have had no quarrel with the latter. He was also accepted by Earls Leofric and Siward; and it was the misfortunes suffered by these two families which enabled the Godwins to establish a collective position even greater than that which their father himself had enjoyed.

Siward had never interfered in the affairs of southern England unless invited by the king so to do. In 1054, at Edward's behest, he invaded Scotland with a large army in support of a claimant to the throne, Malcolm, who had lived long in exile at the English royal court as a hostage, and he was supported on his east flank by a naval squadron.[5] On 27 July he defeated King Macbeth in battle, killed many of his troops and captured much booty. But in the battle fell also Siward's son, Osbeorn,

and his sister's son, another Siward. Moreover, in the following year, on 26 March, the earl himself died at York. As his
only surviving son, Waltheof, was still a boy, some other had
to be found to govern the turbulent frontier earldom. The
post was probably desired by Earl Leofric's son, Ælfgar, at the
time earl of East Anglia. If he were to be chosen, Tostig could
replace him. This arrangement would consolidate the Godwins
in the south and give the Mercian family enormous power
in the north. Neither the queen nor Harold could allow it;
and Edward made Tostig earl of Northumbria.[6] It was a
stupendous increase in the Godwins' territorial power. But
as Tostig seems to have been inexperienced in government
and ruled badly in his earldom, it proved a disaster for the
Godwins, for it contributed to Harold's defeat and death at
Hastings.

The one other major earl, Leofric of Mercia, began to suffer
from the behaviour, or treatment, of his son Ælfgar, earl of
East Anglia since 1053.[7] It must have been difficult for Ælfgar
to establish himself in that territory where the aristocracy, both
lay and clerical, inevitably retained some loyalty to their former
lord, Harold. In 1055 Ælfgar was outlawed by a great royal
council convened about 19 March at a site unknown. Chronicle 'C', followed by John of Worcester, claims that he was
innocent of any crime; 'D' alleges that he had committed hardly
any crime; and 'E' states that he was charged with being a
traitor to the king and all the people of the country — moreover, that he had admitted this in the council, although the
words had escaped him against his will. As it was at this council
that Edward granted Northumbria to Tostig, it may be suspected that Ælfgar had coveted it and may well have enlisted
allies in his support. Also, about this time Edward put the next
of Godwin's sons, Gyrth, in charge of Norfolk, one of Ælfgar's
shires, which would have exacerbated relations between the two
families.[8] Alternatively, the Godwins or their supporters could

have trumped up some charges in order to get the Mercian out of East Anglia.

Guilty or not guilty, the victim then imitated the Godwins by raising forces in Ireland and then Wales, where King Gruffydd ap Llywelyn joined him in person.[9] Gruffydd was the only king ever to rule over the whole of Wales. When in October 1055 the allies attacked Hereford, Earl Ralf gave battle. But his novel cavalry tactics were not a success — to the glee of the insular chronicler — and his troops suffered heavy casualties. The invaders then sacked the episcopal city of Hereford and burnt down the cathedral after killing the canons and stealing the treasures and other relics. Harold led an army raised from all regions to Gloucester, but failed to bring Ælfgar amd Gruffydd to battle. Instead, he fortified Hereford by ringing it with a deep ditch and providing it with gates, no doubt fortified. Finally, at Billingsley in Archenfield in south Herefordshire, still in the Welsh march, Harold made peace with Ælfgar and his allies, and the king reinstated him in his earldom of East Anglia. Harold would not pursue a vendetta against the Mercian family. On 31 August 1056 Earl Odda of Deerhurst, a man against whom no one had a bad word to say, died, after becoming a monk *ad succurrendum* at Pershore Abbey in Worcestershire.[10] His shires in the Welsh march seem to have reverted to Leofric of Mercia.[11]

Vita provides a fairly detailed and quite persuasive appreciation of Harold on the occasion of his succeeding his father in Wessex.[12] It saw him primarily as a soldier. Harold was a second Judas Maccabaeus, the Jewish leader (d. 161 BC) who won spectacular victories over the Syrians and whose deeds are commemorated in the Book of Maccabees, which can be read in the Apocrypha of the English Bible. Harold, a true and even more active son of his father, was notable for the strength of his body and mind. There is one anecdote, however, which implies that he was not very tall.[13] According to the thirteenth-century sagas of the kings of Norway, Harold Sigurdsson (Hardrada), speaking to his ally Earl Tostig before the battle of Stamford Bridge in 1066, remarked of his namesake, the new king of England whom they had just encountered: 'What a little man that was; but he stood proudly in his stirrups.' Hardrada, however, was a giant; and, according to *Vita*, Harold was taller than Tostig. Harold was also remembered in connection with falconry, and indeed is usually shown on the Bayeux Tapestry with a hawk on his wrist. According to Adelard of Bath, the early twelfth-century philosopher and translator and popularizer of Arabic science, who wrote a book on falconry, he had learnt much about the employment of hawks from the books of King Harold.[14] And as likely as not this was the library of Harold Godwinson, which could have fallen into the hands of his Norman successors, for Adelard was for a time in the household of King Henry I.

Vita also commemorates Harold as a governor. He ruled his earldom with patience and mercy, showing kindness to all men of good will, but offering a stern face to thieves and robbers. To study the characters and policies of the princes of Gaul in the interest of English diplomacy he travelled abroad. And from his research he discerned 'what he could get from them in the management of any business'; and 'he acquired such an extensive knowledge of them that he could not be deceived by any of their proposals'. We know that he was at Saint-Omer in November 1056 and in Picardy and Normandy in 1064 or 1065. The earlier trip could have been on the outward or inward journey to Rome which *Vita* believes he made,[15] but it could be connected with the search for Edmund Ironside's descendants which was in progress at this time.[16] *Vita* does not make it clear in whose interests Harold's diplomacy was conducted. Although the earl, like many other leading men in the kingdom — and the queen — must have had the problem of the succession to the throne often on his mind, it would seem unlikely that in the 1050s he was already planning to succeed his brother-in-law.

Vita also compares and contrasts Harold and Tostig. Both were handsome and graceful men, equally strong and brave. But Harold was the taller and had had much experience of the hardships of military campaigns. He was also milder in temper and more intelligent than Tostig. He could suffer contradiction well and would seldom retaliate, and on a compatriot never. Tostig too could show restraint, although he was occasionally over-zealous in attacking evil. Harold shared his plans with loyal men and sometimes deferred action so long that some might think it was to his disadvantage. Tostig, on the other hand, was secretive and disinclined to share his plans with others, so that his actions were unexpected — which was advantageous to him. But, as would be expected of sons of Godwin, neither was rash or irresolute. Both persevered with what they had begun. Harold, aiming at happiness, acted prudently; Tostig, aiming solely at success, acted vigorously. Both could dissemble and puzzle the observer. Harold 'by God's grace, came home safely, passing through all ambushes with watchful mockery as was his way'. Before the final disaster he was invulnerable.

Some qualities the encomiast gave to Tostig he obviously withheld from Harold. Tostig was faithful to his noble wife and decent in his language. Elsewhere Harold is said to have been prodigal with oaths. Tostig was generous with gifts, and these, at the prompting of his religious wife, were more often to the church than to other men. Foreign writers, anxious to demonize Harold, accuse him of promiscuity and adultery.[17] The English Coleman, however (Bishop Wulfstan's chaplain and biographer), asserts that he was a close friend of Wulfstan, the monastic and most religious bishop of Worcester, later deemed a saint.[18]

Harold seems indeed to have entered into no Christian or dynastic marriage before he became king; but it would appear that, from his time as earl of East Anglia, he had a relatively stable relationship with a Norfolk noblewoman, Edith Swan-neck, who may also have been known as Edith the Fair and Edith the Rich.[19] She could have been the daughter of a woman named Wulfgyth, who made her will in 1046. It is generally believed that it was a 'hand-fast' union, a marriage *more danico*, that is to say one unblessed by the church, such as King Cnut's with Ælfgifu of Northampton, and one which would not preclude a later Christian marriage. According to Domesday Book Edith and her men held in the five shires of Hertfordshire, Buckinghamshire, Suffolk, Essex and Cambridgeshire nearly 280 hides and 450 acres of land, the most in Cambridgeshire. The whole was a considerable endowment.[20]

Edward Bulwer-Lytton, in his historical novel, *Harold, the Last of the Saxon Kings* (1848), makes Edith Harold's one and only love, but impossible to marry without an ecclesiastical dispensation since they were related in the fifth degree.[21] She lived with her grandmother, a pagan witch named Hilda, and was also a godchild of Harold's sister, the queen. There seems to be no evidence for any of these suppositions. Lytton presumably invented them to excuse Harold's failure to make an honest woman of her, although he loved her with a love that was pure and Christian. Five children have been attributed to this union: three boys, Godwin, Edmund and Magnus, and two daughters, Gytha and Gunhild. The names are eclectic but with a Scandinavian bias. Godwin was, of course, called after his grandfather, Edmund presumably after Edmund Ironside, Magnus after the king of Norway, Gytha after her grandmother and Gunhild after her aunt. One unbaptised child of theirs, perhaps stillborn, was buried in Christ Church, Canterbury, next to St Dunstan's tomb. The post-Conquest Canterbury monks, Osbert and Eadmer, remembered this profanity with horror.[22]

There is also a tradition that the man who buried Harold after the battle of Hastings was William Malet, named only by

Plate 1
Edward, type 9; crowned bust facing. Photo © B. Wilson/Ancient Art and Architecture Collection Ltd.

Plate 2

Harold (in front, carrying hawk) rides to Bosham church and hall. The Bayeux Tapestry – XIth century. By special permission of the City of Bayeux.

(Plate 2 continued)

Plate 3
Harold (in front) is escorted by Duke William (carrying hawk) to
his palace at Rouen. The Bayeux Tapestry – XIth century. By special
permission of the City of Bayeux.

Plate 4

The mysterious event at the ducal palace at Rouen, involving the clerk and Ælfgyva. The Bayeux Tapestry – XIth century. By special permission of the City of Bayeux.

Plate 5
William knights Harold after their successful Breton campaign. The
Bayeux Tapestry – XIth century. By special permission of the City
of Bayeux.

Plate 6
Harold takes an oath to the seated Duke William. The Bayeux
Tapestry – XIth century. By special permission of the City of
Bayeux.

Plate 7
Harold returns to England. Edward dies on 4/5 January 1066 and on
6 January is buried in Westminster Abbey which he has rebuilt. The
Bayeux Tapestry – XIth century. By special permission of the City of
Bayeux.

(Plate 7 continued)

Plate 8
Harold is killed, 14 October 1066. The Bayeux Tapestry – XIth century.
By special permission of the City of Bayeux.

(Plate 8 continued)

Plate 9
Harold; crowned bust to left with sceptre.
Photo © C M Dixon

William of Poitiers and described in Guy of Amiens's poem on the battle as half-English, half-Norman and Harold's *compater*.[23] This should mean that William had an English mother and that he and Harold had been co-sponsors at a baptism. The Malets were a Norman family from Graville-Sainte-Honorine at the mouth of the Seine, who are first noticed after the Norman Conquest when William and his son Robert had a large estate in East Anglia, with the *caput* at Eye in Suffolk. But so far no evidence has been found that a Malet was in England before 1066; indeed William's ancestry is a complete mystery. Hence his connection with Harold must remain in doubt.

Which of the two brothers, Harold and Tostig, the author of *Vita* preferred is also not perfectly clear. He obviously admired Harold and was aware of Tostig's faults. But he knew more about the younger brother. Whereas he dismisses Harold's pilgrimage to Rome in a few words, he devotes a disproportionate attention to Tostig's. It may also be thought that Queen Edith preferred Tostig. A Norman writer alleges that she did not support Harold's seizure of the throne in 1066.[24] Although it is increasingly hinted in *Vita* that there was rivalry between the two brothers and that this led to the tragic end of the story, it would not seem that there was trouble in the period 1055–65.

It is useless to look for realistic representations of eleventh-century people. When featured, artistic stereotypes are the norm. But it is worthwhile enquiring whether anything can be learnt from the images of some of Godwin's children which appear on the Bayeux Tapestry. As this was designed and manufactured at Canterbury probably in the late 1070s when most of the earl's children were dead, and their likenesses cannot have been generally known, expectations cannot be high. Harold Godwinson appears quite often, but his face, apart from his moustaches, is nondescript. He is, however, portrayed as blond. On his coinage his face is shown in profile with a slightly aquiline nose, a short beard and possibly a small moustache.

His brothers, Gyrth and Leofwine, appear once on the tapestry, completely disguised by armour. It is likely that all three are artistically idealized as elegant warriors. Women are rarely featured on the tapestry, Queen Edith only once and unidentified, weeping at King Edward's deathbed, almost completely muffled. If the Ælfgifu of an earlier enigmatic scene is indeed her sister, she too is carefully obscured. Godwin's son-in-law, King Edward, from first to last appears on the tapestry stereotyped as an ancient and wise ruler with a long beard. It would seem, therefore, that in none of these cases were there remembered individual features which an artist could emphasize or caricature.

After 1055, with Harold guarding the south and Tostig the north, the king, under the direction of the queen, could devote his time to hunting and good works. From 1055 Edith regularly witnessed royal charters, always at the top of the list after the king. The Scandinavian threat had faded after the death of Magnus of Norway in 1047; and the hostility of Flanders was mitigated when Duke William of Normandy married Matilda, the daughter of Count Baldwin V, probably in 1052. The marriage also brought William into a distant family relationship with Tostig.

Harold's main problem in England was the turbulence of Ælfgar of Mercia, earl of East Anglia, and the hostility of his ally, Gruffydd ap Llywelyn, who had made himself ruler of the whole of Wales and was to become one of the heroes of Welsh history. The English government was also giving fresh thought to the problem of the succession. An 'English' party, to which Harold was probably sympathetic, in order to defeat the claims of Swegen of Denmark and William of Normandy, began to search for descendants of King Æthelred, especially the children of his son, Edmund Ironside, king in 1016. These, Edward and Edmund, had found their way to Hungary when Cnut had seized the English throne in 1016. Edmund had died there, but Edward 'the Exile' had married a woman named Agatha, who was certainly related to the German king and emperor, Henry II, and may have been the daughter of King Stephen of Hungary, the saint (995–1038).[25] Edward had acquired an important position at the Magyar court and he and his wife had three children, Margaret the future queen of Scots, Christina, later a nun, and Edgar 'the atheling', all of them young in the 1050s.

In the later summer of 1054 Edward sent Bishop Ealdred of Worcester on an embassy to the German king, Henry III, presumably to inaugurate the search.[26] The English monarchy had a connection with the German, for Cnut and Emma's daughter, Gunhild, had married in 1036 King Conrad's son, Henry, the future Emperor Henry III. Although she died without issue three years later and Henry remarried, he seems to have retained an interest in England for he is credited with sending a physician to cure Harold Godwinson of some disease. In 1054 Ealdred, after staying at Cologne for a year, returned empty-handed. Henry III was on bad terms with Andrew I king of Hungary (1046–1061); communications were, therefore, difficult; and Edward the Exile cannot have been eager to return. The German king died on 5 October 1056, and it seems as though the English royal court immediately made a new move. Harold was at Saint-Omer on 13 November 1056 when he witnessed a charter of his brother-in-law, Count Baldwin V.[27] And it has been conjectured that he then accompanied Baldwin to the German court at Cologne, where he would have met not only the regent, the formidable Agnes of Poitou, Henry's widow,[28] with her young son Henry IV, but also Pope Victor II. He may then have gone with the court to Regensburg on the Danube, from where he could have negotiated with Hungary. And in the meantime he could even have travelled to Rome with the pope, before returning to Bavaria and picking up Edward the Exile for conveyance to England.

The only hard evidence for these long journeys is Harold's presence at Saint-Omer. But *Vita* states baldly that Harold, like Tostig, visited Rome,[29] and it was remembered at Harold's foundation at Waltham that he had been to the holy city. In the early-thirteenth-century fictional *Vita Haroldi* it is stated that the earl went there to collect relics for his college and that four or five days out on his return journey he was caught up by Romans indignant that he had despoiled the city of so much treasure, and forced to disgorge much of it. This can be compared with Tostig's better-attested misfortune after leaving Rome. Certainly Waltham came into possession of relics which Harold could have collected on such an itinerary from Saint-Omer.[30] And that his activities in this period are not noticed in the chronicle can be variously interpreted.

However all this may be, in the spring of 1057 Edward returned to England, only to die on 19 April before he had even seen the king. He was buried in St Paul's, London. He seems to have returned with his whole family. What happened to Agatha is unknown; but their offspring appear to have been brought up at the royal court. *Vita*, without providing names, in his eulogy of Edith refused to pass over in silence 'how zealously she reared, educated, adorned and showered with motherly love those children who were said to be of royal stock'.[31] She had indeed preserved the Old-English royal line, which was to reappear in England when, on 11 November 1100, King Henry I married Matilda, daughter of King Malcolm III (Canmore) of Scots and his wife Margaret, Edward the Exile's daughter. With the return of Edward the Exile's family in 1057 the problem of the succession could well have been considered settled. That the king allowed Edgar, Edward's son, the title of *atheling* shows that he was regarded as throneworthy.[32] In effect, Edward and Edith adopted him as a son; and Edgar was ineffectually elected king after Harold's death. His youth — he was no more than five in 1057 — was not reassuring. Yet the king was to live for another nine years and Edgar, after an adventurous career, survived perhaps until 1120.

The deaths of Earls Leofric of Mercia in the autumn of 1057 and Ralf of Hereford on 21 December raised the problems not only of the redistribution of the earldoms but also of the English defences against the Welsh. Leofric had not been one of the great movers and shakers — indeed he is best remembered for his wife, the Lady Godiva — but had certainly been a man totally loyal to the king and the kingdom's welfare. Both he and Ralf had been on good terms with the Godwins. And in both cases there was a difficulty over the succession. Leofric's son, Ælfgar, earl of East Anglia, had caused trouble in the past, especially because of his alliance, mentioned above, with Gruffydd of Wales. And Ralf's son and heir, Harold, was a child. The king allowed Ælfgar to succeed his father; and the Godwins divided up the rest. Harold's brother, Gyrth, took over the whole of East Anglia and was also active in Oxfordshire. The next sibling, Leofwine, was given southeastern England, the shires round the mouth of the Thames. He features in Domesday Book far less prominently than Gyrth. As for Herefordshire, which seems to have included part of Gloucestershire and perhaps Shropshire, it was annexed by Harold, but possibly only as a temporary expedient until his namesake, possibly his godson, should come of age. This boy was still in Queen Edith's wardship in 1066.[33] As E.A. Freeman justly remarked, 'the house of Godwin had thus reached the greatest height of power and dignity which a subject house could reach; . . . they had won for themselves a position such as no English family ever won before or after . . . The whole kingdom, save a few shires in the middle, was in their hands.'[34] Indeed, momentarily it seemed that the whole of England was theirs, for shortly after Ælfgar moved to Mercia, he was banished from the kingdom.[35]

The value of the estates held by the Godwins, other earls and the king in 1066 can be calculated (roughly) from Domesday

Book. For most of the manors listed the survey names the tenant 'on the day King Edward was alive and dead', and provides its rateable value (expressed in hides or carucates) and its monetary value. Totals can, therefore, be calculated, and several historians have produced these.[36] Although there are discrepancies between them, the general picture is clear: the Godwins were certainly by far the wealthiest family after the king, perhaps even overtopping him, and in 1066 Harold was the richest member of the family.

Using Domesday statistics, the wealth of the landowners can be presented in one of two ways: as an aggregate either of the rateable values of the manors or of the monetary values of these. Although the former convey better the spatial dimension of the estate, the hidage was an arbitrary allotment and could easily be changed by royal action, whereas the monetary value, it is believed, was a realistic estimate of the revenue the manor yielded annually to its lord. Figures can be produced for Earl Godwin, his wife Gytha, and their children Harold, Tostig, Gyrth, Leofwine and Gunhild. But not everything is straightforward. Whether Queen Edith's vast estate should go with the Godwins or the royal demesne is debatable, although they seem to have been derived largely from the latter. Whether the lands of Edith Swan-neck should be added to Harold's is likewise a matter of opinion. And who held in 1066 the lands credited to Godwin, who had died in 1053, is unknown and unknowable. But on any interpretation of these matters the Godwins emerge as a family, and Harold as an individual, as outstandingly wealthy. The family estate was valued at around £7,000, with Harold's share at least £5,000. In contrast, the estates of Earl Leofric's family were valued at £2,400, Earl Siward's at £350 and Earl Ralf's at £170. The royal demesne was valued at around £5,000. Missing from these figures, however, are the values of all sorts of rights and services which lords of vassals enjoyed. And it is likely that the king was the greatest beneficiary of these.

Using the alternative figures, the rateable value of the manors, Harold held something more than 1,900 hides, nearly 500 carucates and 3 sulungs of land. To this can be added the lands of his vassals. His largest holdings were in Wessex itself, in Sussex, Berkshire, Dorset, Wiltshire, Surrey, Cornwall, Devon and Somerset; and he also had large estates in Herefordshire, Gloucestershire, Lincolnshire, Hampshire and Essex, then part of East Anglia. He even held lands in Yorkshire. In other words, he possessed most land in the earldoms which he had once held. But he had also picked up estates in Mercia, the East Midlands and Northumbria. This vast holding had come to him from several directions. Some parts were his share of the family lands and some were attached to the comital office or had been royal demesne. The lands in Mercia could mostly have come from his second marriage to Edwin and Morcar's sister. To these were added gifts and bequests and the lands of men who commended themselves to him — his clientèle or vassalage. There were also, inevitably, some 'illegal' acquisitions, especially from churches. The value of the latter has been put at more than £342. But it was easy in 1086 for churches to claim that they had been robbed of these lands: leases, to which they were prone, could easily go astray.

This immense accumulation of wealth in the hands of the Godwins has led Robin Fleming to judge: 'If the Confessor approved the family's aggrandizement and its vast network of allies, he was a fool; if he acquiesced, he cannot have been in full control of the kingdom. Domesday Book, therefore, offers damning evidence against the competence of Edward the Confessor and the stability of his régime.'[37] But, since Edward tried to get rid of the whole family in 1051, he could not have approved, and since after the failure of that coup he accepted the dominance of his wife's family he showed himself a realist. The power of the Godwins, when at the disposal of the king and queen, provided the monarchy with stability. They held lands in most of the coastal areas vulnerable to attacks by vikings, other predators and foreign enemies, especially in the southeast and the Isle of Wight, as well as estates in the Welsh marches. And although this strong position did not sustain Harold for long, the family's confiscated estates richly endowed the Norman monarchy.

How this agglomeration of scattered estates was administered is unknown, except that at the lowest level individual manors or holdings were, in the usual way, in the charge of reeves.[38] Whether Harold imitated the king by appointing shire-reeves (sheriffs) to supervise these, is unknown. But it is likely that, as with the royal demesne and most large ecclesiastical estates, manors were organized into either provisioning or revenue units. Central control must have been provided in Harold's household, although of this we know nothing. What we can also assume is that the earl was constantly on the move, moving from one of his estates to another, consuming the provender of the provisioning units and collecting money from their revenue counterparts.

His itineraries are unascertainable. We cannot even identify his favourite residences. He should have presided over the shire courts at least twice a year and heard cases and done royal business there; and it is possible that, as he governed many shires, their courts were grouped at provincial centres, so as to make his attendance feasible. As he would have led a sizeable retinue on his travels, his visitations may not have been always warmly welcomed. The households of some kings and nobles behaved like bandits. But the eulogies that Harold earned suggest that he kept his under control.

Inevitably the Godwins could not retain all that they had amassed by 1057, when Earls Leofric and Ralf died. It is even possible that Harold saw little point in increasing his share. Although he had heavy outgoings in the 1050s, when he was establishing his college at Waltham — and the magnificence of this foundation shows the magnitude of his wealth — there must have come the point, even for him, at which more property became a further burden. This can be seen from his treatment of the Mercian family. The expulsion of Earl Ælfgar in 1057, shortly after he had taken over Mercia, repeats that of 1055; and the standing reason for the suspicion with which Ælfgar was regarded may be his close ties with Gruffydd ap Llywelyn. It was about this time, it is thought, that he gave his daughter, Ealdgyth, in marriage to the Welsh prince, described by Alfred Lord Tennyson as 'the nimble, wild, red, wiry, savage king'.[39] They had one daughter, Nest, who married the marcher lord Osbern fitz Richard, of Richard's Castle on the Herefordshire/Shropshire border. Moreover, as in 1055, Ælfgar was able to return with Gruffydd's help, aided this time by a viking fleet under the command of one no less than Magnus, the son of Harold Sigurdsson (Hardrada), king of Norway. This expedition, operating off the west coast of Britain, would seem to have been aimed at conquest, like that of Harold Hardrada himself in 1066 and those earlier of the Danish adventurers, Swegen and Cnut. But all that the combined forces achieved in 1058 was Ælfgar's restoration to Mercia. Harold may have bought the invasion off with this. Chronicle 'D' exclaims: 'It is tedious to relate fully how things went.' It can only be thought that Harold and the royal court were buying time. Harold often seems like his father in his reluctance to force a showdown, in preferring diplomacy and compromise to war. It may be, of course, that in 1058 he lacked the resources for facing up to Ælfgar and his foreign allies. However that may be, in the following peaceful years the Godwins consolidated their position.

Tostig may be considered to have had the most difficult task. The Northumbrian aristocracy, in which Scandinavian blood and culture predominated, cannot have relished the rule of a West-Saxon earl. It was also one of the most lawless areas and was coveted by the king of Scots, all the more since Siward, by defeating Macbeth (who died in 1057) had prepared the way for Malcolm III (Canmore), a much more anglicized prince, to take the throne in 1058. According to *Vita*, Tostig cultivated his friendship;[40] and certainly in 1059, probably at Christmas, the earl, together with Ealdred archbishop of York and Æthelwine bishop of Durham, conducted the king to Edward's court at Gloucester.[41] Malcolm made peace and gave hostages. So confident was Tostig of his hold over Northumbria that he seems often to have been at the English royal court, a habit which suggests that his relations with the queen, his sister, were close. And in 1061 he led an important legation to the papal curia which is described at length in *Vita*.[42] These absences were possible because he had a capable deputy, Copsig,[43] who was briefly to be earl in Northumbria after the Norman Conquest.

Vita claims that Tostig was very stern to law-breakers; and apparently he introduced some West-Saxon laws — presumably those hostile to feuds and lawlessness — into his earldom.[44] But, however laudable his attempt to subdue a refractory province may have been, *Vita*'s remark that he was sometimes overzealous in attacking evil suggests that he could act unwisely. Certainly he himself got involved in feuds, and his rule became generally unpopular. He and his wife Judith were, however, regarded as benefactors of the church. In the Durham *Liber Vitae*, a catalogue of its patrons, TOSTI is written in letters of gold.[45]

The embassy to Rome was a consequence of the promotion of Bishop Ealdred of Worcester to the archbishopric of York at Christmas 1060. He not only required a pallium, the livery of his office, from Pope Nicholas II (1058–61), he would also have to explain how he had come to hold several bishoprics in plurality and transfer now from one diocese to another without papal permission. Also in his company were the clerks Giso and

Walter, the one requiring consecration to Wells, the other to Hereford, which they could not obtain in England because of the doubtful legality of Stigand at Canterbury. And there were some other clerical litigants in the party. On the lay side, Tostig was accompanied by his wife and his younger brother, Gyrth. A Northumbrian nobleman, Gospatric, is also found in the company; and there would have been a military escort as well. Whether Tostig had any royal business to transact is not clear. But they travelled via 'Saxony and the upper reaches of the Rhine', possibly by way of Cologne and Mainz, before crossing Burgundy and the Alps into Lombardy, a more northerly route than usual, and one suggesting contact with the German and even the Hungarian courts. They are credited with devoutly visiting all the shrines en route, and arrived at Rome before Easter (15 April).

At Pope Nicholas's Easter synod, which attacked simoniacs but is not known to have issued laws, the pope seated Tostig next to himself. But Ealdred's business did not go so well, and with the main matter on hold, Tostig dispatched Judith with most of his retinue to return home; and they reached England safely by an unstated route. Finally, the pope not only refused Ealdred the pallium but also deprived him of his episcopal orders, thus depriving him of both York and Worcester. Tostig angrily threatened Nicholas with non-payment in future of Peter's Pence, the annual tribute England had for centuries rendered Rome, and which the earl had probably brought with him. But to no avail. And the embassy's tribulations were not over. As they rode off, they were, perhaps on the same day, intercepted by the Tuscan nobleman, Gerard count of Galeria, an enemy of the pope, probably where the road from Galeria meets the Via Cassia in the most desolate stretch of the Campagna. The quick thinking of Gospatric, who was in the van and pretended to be the earl, allowed them to escape with their lives if not their money and other possessions. And on returning to Rome, their plight, and perhaps the fear of even rougher threats from Tostig, persuaded the pope to be merciful. The earl was loaded with gifts, Ealdred was reinstated and granted the pallium, but only on condition that he resigned Worcester; and the pope sent cardinals, who probably travelled with the English party, to see that the condition was observed and also to investigate the state of the English church.

Some of the party were still in Rome towards the end of July when Pope Nicholas died and was succeeded at the end of September by Alexander II. Ealdred was certainly back at Worcester by Lent 1062; and it is likely that both he and Tostig travelled back in the autumn of 1061 without further mishap. As Tostig and Ealdred would have had to report to the king, the earl's absence from his earldom must have been the best part of a year. During that time Malcolm king of Scots had raided deep into Northumbria. But Tostig apparently regarded it as no breach of their treaty and restored good relations. There was to be peace with Scotland for the remainder of Edward's reign.

Notes

1. Migne, J.P. (ed.) (1844) *Patrologiae cursus completus, Patrologia latina*, 221 vols. Paris, cxcv, col. 763.
2. Barlow, *Edward*, appendix B, pp. 301–6.
3. Hariulf of Saint-Riquier, *Chronicon Cetulense*, ed. F. Lot, Collection des Textes pour servir à l'étude et à l'enseignement de l'histoire (Paris, 1894), pp. 237–8.
4. For her household see Stafford, pp. 107–22.
5. Barlow, *Edward*, p. 202.
6. *Vita*, pp. 48–9; *ASC, s.a.*
7. *ASC, s.a.*
8. *Vita*, pp. 50–1.
9. Lloyd, *Wales*, pp. 364 ff. K.L. Maund, 'The Welsh alliances of Earl Ælfgar of Mercia', *ANS*, xi (1989), 181–90.

10. *ASC*, 'C', 'D'.
11. *FNC*, ii. 581–2.
12. *Vita*, pp. 46–53.
13. Snorri Sturluson, *Heimskringla*, ed. S. Laing (2nd edn 1880); *King Harald's Saga*, cap. 91. *Vita*, pp. 48–9.
14. See above, p. 34 and note 39.
15. *Vita*, pp. 52–3; see Körner, pp. 205–6.
16. See below, pp. 81–3.
17. *Carmen*, v. 261; *GG*, ii, 8, ed. Chibnall, pp. 114–15.
18. *Vita Wulfstani*, pp. 13, 18, 22–4. For the benevolence of Godwin and Harold towards the see of Worcester, see A. Williams, 'The spoliation of Worcester', *ANS*, xix (1997), 400.
19. *FNC*, ii, appendix RR, and iv, appendix M; *EHD*, ii, no. 187, pp. 903–4; E. Searle, 'Women and the legitimization of succession at the Norman Conquest', *ANS*, iii (1981), 161–2. She may, however, be 'Harold's Concubine' who held 4 messuages in Canterbury, *DB*, i. 2.
20. A. Williams, 'The estates of Harold Godwineson', *ANS*, iii (1981), pp. 161–2; Walker, p. 61.
21. P. 160.
22. *Memorials of St Dunstan, archbishop of Canterbury*, ed. W. Stubbs (Rolls ser. 1874), pp. 141–2, 230.
23. *Carmen*, vv. 587–8, pp. 34–5; *GG*, ii, 25, ed. Chibnall, pp. 140–1; V. Brown, *Rye Priory Cartulary and Charters*, Suffolk Records Soc., 2 vols, ii (1994), 4–7; C.R. Hart, 'William Malet and his family', *ANS*, xix (1997), 123–65.
24. *GG*, ii, 8, ed. Chibnall, pp. 114–15. She certainly came to terms with the Conqueror and enjoyed her dower lands until her death in 1075.
25. For the controversy over whether Agatha was a German or Hungarian princess, see Barlow, *Edward*, p. 216, n. 2. Hungarian history is very complicated at this time and because of the twelfth-century Gaimar's inventions in his *Lestoire des Engleis*, some very strange accounts of Æthelred's descendants are in circulation. One takes Edward the Confessor to Hungary and a (second) marriage to Agatha, a daughter of King Stephen: William N. Austin (privately circulated). A 'history' of Edward 'the Exile' is Gabriel Ronay, *The Lost King of England* (1989).
26. *ASC, s.a.*
27. P. Grierson, 'A visit of Earl Harold to Flanders in 1056', *EHR*, li (1936), 90–7; and above, n. 15.

28. For Agnes, see R.W. Southern, *The Making of the Middle Ages*, Hutchinson, London (1953), pp. 76–8.

29. *Vita*, pp. 52–3.

30. *Vita Haroldi*, trans, Swanton, pp. 17–18; M.E.C. Walcot, 'Inventory of Waltham Holy Cross', *Trans. Essex Arch. Soc.*, v (1873), 257–64, at p. 261.

31. *Vita*, pp. 24–5.

32. For the significance of the title, see Stafford, pp. 76, 82–3, 269.

33. *DB*, i. 129b.

34. *FNC*, ii. 428–9.

35. *ASC*, 'D', *s.a.* 1058; Lloyd, *Wales*, ii. 368–9.

36. *FNC*, ii, *passim*; Robert H. Davies, 'The lands and rights of Harold son of Godwine, and their distribution by William I. A study in the Domesday evidence.' (Unpublished M.A. Diss., University College, Cardiff, 1967.) A. Williams, 'Land and power in the eleventh century: the estates of Harold Godwineson', *ANS*, iii (1981), 171–87; R. Fleming, 'Domesday estates of the king and the Godwinesons: a study in late Saxon politics', *Speculum*, lviii (1983), 254–76; idem, *Kings and Lords in Conquest England* (1991), Cambridge University Press, Cambridge; P.A. Clarke, *The English Nobility under Edward the Confessor* (1994); Walker, ch. 4. For Edith, Stafford, pp. 123–42, 280–305, and Fig. 4; J.L. Grassi, 'The lands and revenues of Edward the Confessor', *EHR* 117 (2002), 251–83.

37. R. Fleming, *Kings and Lords in Conquest England* (1991), Cambridge University Press, p. 102; cf. idem in *Speculum*, lviii, 1007.

38. See Barlow, *Edward*, ch. 7. Some of Harold's reeves are mentioned in *DB*, i. 298, ii. 5a–b.

39. *Harold: a Drama*: Act IV, sc. 1, p. 106.

40. *Vita*, pp. 66–7.

41. Barlow, *Edward*, p. 203.

42. *Vita*, pp. 52–7; *Vita Wulfstani*, pp. 16–17.

43. Symeon of Durham, *Historia Ecclesiae Dunelmensis*, ed. T. Arnold (Rolls ser., 1882), p. 97.

44. Barlow, *Edward*, p. 235.

45. Durham's *Liber Vitae*, fo. 12ᵛ, Surtees Soc., xiii (1841), p. 2. See also Symeon, *Historia Ecclesiae Dunelmensis*, ed. T. Arnold (Rolls ser., 1882), i. 94–5.

chapter 5

THE LULL BEFORE THE STORMS, 1062–1065

With Harold established in Wessex and Tostig in Northumbria, *Vita* hails:

> *These two great brothers of a cloud-born land,*
> *The kingdom's sacred oaks, two Hercules,*
> *Excel all Englishmen when joined in peace;*
> *And as of yore the sky's divided weight*
> *Was held by Atlas here, Heracles there,*
> *Lest heaven fall and earth sink all around,*
> *So these angelic Angles with joined strength*
> *And like agreement guard the English bounds.*[1]

The danger to England from foreign princes and adventurers seemed to be in decline, and the king, encouraged by his consort, devoted himself to hunting and a great religious foundation. The several versions of *The Anglo-Saxon Chronicle* show minimal interest in foreign and even national affairs. 'E' alone notices, in a Latin entry, William of Normandy's conquest of Maine in 1062 (probably a mistake for 1063). None records the defeat of Swegen of Denmark by Harold Hardrada of Norway in the battle of Nissa in 1062, or the peace they subsequently made at Gota in 1064. The death of King Edward's last surviving nephew, Walter III, count of Mantes, in 1064 went unnoticed. Even the death of Earl Ælfgar of Mercia, which must have occurred about 1062, gets no mention. Perhaps, even more significant, Harold's ill-fated visit to Normandy in 1064 or 1065 is ignored by all except foreign writers. All these matters must have seemed too tedious to record[2] — or too irrelevant in view of later events.

Ælfgar of Mercia left two sons, Edwin and Morcar, both probably in their early teens; and the elder, Edwin, was made earl in his father's place by the king, probably acting in council. As all the available sons of Earl Godwin by then held earldoms, they could afford to rein in their greed. It was Gruffydd ap Llywelyn who was most affected by this event.[3] He had been Ælfgar's friend and now felt that his hands were free again, especially since Ralf of Hereford also was dead. But it was equally an opportunity for Harold, who developed into a true Welsh marcher lord. In 1056 his clerk, Leofgar, had been appointed bishop of Hereford, a warrior who, to the chronicler's disgust, wore moustaches until ordained bishop.[4] And on 16 June, shortly after his consecration, he led an army against Gruffydd only to be heavily defeated and killed, probably at Glasbury-on-Wye. With the bishop fell also some of his priests, the sheriff and many thegns. In the end Earls Leofric and Harold negotiated a peace, whereby Gruffydd swore that he would be a faithful under-king to Edward and in return was confirmed in his possessions. These were not only the several Welsh principalities under his control but also the fringe of conquests at the expense of English settlers. Welsh expansion was halted, and the peace held for a time. Bishop Ealdred of Worcester, who after Leofgar's death added the diocese of Hereford to his charge, was able to leave those two bishoprics untenanted for at least six months in 1058 while he made a pilgrimage to Jerusalem.[5] But the defeats probably rankled with

Harold, who had been in charge of Herefordshire since 1057, and thus the lord of Ewyas Harold, Hereford and Richard's Castle, three of the few pre-Conquest castles in England.

Although Gruffydd was married to the new earl of Mercia's sister, after Ælfgar's death the Welsh began raiding again; and at Edward's Christmas court, held as usual at Gloucester in 1062, it was decided to act decisively against the Welsh prince.[6] First Harold made a small cavalry raid with household troops which almost surprised Gruffydd in his 'palace' at Rhuddlan on the River Clwyd in north Wales. Then, in May 1063, a full-scale campaign was launched. Tostig invaded north Wales, presumably from Chester, while Harold sailed with a fleet from Bristol to ravage the Welsh coastline and prevent Gruffydd escaping. Although the prince did evade the pincer attack, on 5 August he was killed in Snowdonia by his own men. Meanwhile the two earls received the submission of most of the Welsh nobles. In the end, Gruffydd's head and the prow of his ship were surrendered to Harold, who delivered them in person to the king.[7] It was indeed a great and much celebrated victory.

In what is either the concluding poem of Book I of *Vita* or the opening poem of Book II, the family's encomiast devotes 32 lines to the brother earls' campaign, climaxing in the delivery to Edward of the prow and stern of the ship cast in solid gold, together with other loot and the hostages. Nor was the victory soon forgotten. In the twelfth century Gerald of Wales wrote that Harold had almost exterminated the Welsh and erected stone pillars inscribed with 'Here was Harold the Conqueror', as monuments to his victory.[8] John of Salisbury in his *Policraticus* cited Harold's campaign as an excellent example of that military training required of all nations to keep them healthy and capable of defending themselves. According to the patriotic John, Harold presented the heads of several kings to Edward and killed so many men — all that he could find — that Edward in his mercy gave permission for Welsh women to marry Englishmen. Harold also promulgated a law that any Welshman found with a weapon beyond Offa's Dyke should have his right hand cut off.[9] After this conquest of Wales it was decided that the northern areas should be divided between Gruffydd's two half-brothers, Bleddyn and Rhiwallon; and Harold put them in possession of their parts on condition that they would be faithful vassals of King Edward, perform military service for him on land and sea and pay all the customs that had ever been due from Wales. And it was, apparently, to Harold that they swore oaths and gave hostages to ensure their compliance. As south Wales too was in turmoil, the whole principality had reverted again to disunity. As Geoffrey Gaimar wrote in his *Lestoire des Engleis*: 'After this no one paid any heed to the Welsh.'[10]

The Anglo-Saxon Chronicle is blank for the year 1064 and does not mention Harold again until he invaded south Wales before Lammas (1 August) 1065. It is into this slot that Harold's apparently disastrous visit to Normandy — if indeed it actually occurred — has to be fitted. The Norman chroniclers' insistence that Edward was on his last legs points to 1065; but William of Poitiers's belief that in Brittany the corn was green and there was a dearth of food would suit, perhaps, 1064 better than the following year.[11] This episode, an integral and vital element in the Norman case for the legality of William's claim to succeed Edward on the English throne and the illegality of Harold's usurpation of it, is therefore highly suspect and can be rejected, together with all the other parts of the case, as pure fiction. There is no corroboration from English sources: the versions given by twelfth-century English authors, such as Eadmer and William of Malmesbury, are best regarded as refashionings of the Norman story.[12] There is, however, sufficient support from non-Norman sources to afford it some credibility.

In *Carmen*, which antedates and contributes to the Norman story, Guy, Bishop of Amiens, makes several references to Harold's oath to William in the diplomatic exchanges he ascribes to the two rivals immediately before the Battle of Hastings. William charges Harold with having agreed to Edward's nomination of him as his heir (presumably in 1051), asserts that the earl had delivered to him personally (presumably in 1064–5) important symbols of the bequest, a sword and a ring, and claims that as Harold had disregarded the oaths he had sworn him he was a perjurer. Harold in return complains that William had failed to observe treaties and keep his knightly word.[13] From this it is clear that the story of the visit was current at the time of William's invasion of England and that it was credible to a French bishop and presumably to his nephews, the lords of Ponthieu. The author of *Vita*, writing a little later, believed that Harold investigated in person the attitude of foreign princes, a statement which we have already discussed, and remarks elsewhere that Harold was, alas, too free with oaths.[14] Nor is the silence of all versions of the patriotic chronicle fatal to the story. It is what might be expected. Finally, the complete fabrication of the whole case by the Norman ducal court and its agents would seem an effrontery almost beyond belief.

It can therefore be accepted that some versions of Harold's visit and oath to William were generally current in Europe and that immediately after Edward's death William's apologists incorporated it into the literary case they made for circulation to Pope Alexander II and other European rulers in order to get their sympathy or support for the duke's proposed invasion of England. All the same, the case is an *ex parte* statement which, if not completely false, is bound to be biased and untrustworthy. Even if it be accepted in outline, the detail provided by its several retailers must be viewed with caution.

William of Poitiers provides the fullest exposition of the duke's claim to the English crown.[15] The first plank is the oath of the

English magnates in 1051–2. The second is Harold's visit to
the duke. Edward, when dying, sent Harold to confirm by his
oath the royal promise of the succession. This was done so that
the earl could compel the English people to accept William as
king. Harold escaped some danger as he sailed for Normandy
and landed on the coast of Ponthieu where he fell into the
hands of its count, Guy, who held the English party to ransom.
When William heard of this he persuaded Guy to release them,
received them on the northern border of the duchy at Eu,
and conducted them to Rouen. He was most hospitable to his
guests and in a council at Bonneville-sur-Touques Harold swore
fealty to him. In return, at Harold's request, William confirmed
to his vassal all his lands and other rights. Then Harold, of his
own free will, promised to be William's vicar at Edward's court;
to fortify Dover and such other places as the duke would specify
and garrison them with Norman knights whom he would fully
maintain; and, finally, on Edward's death Harold would get the
duke accepted as king. Much later in the book the archdeacon
of Lisieux remarks that William had not wanted the death of
Harold but rather his marriage to his daughter. Orderic Vitalis
embroiders this by claiming that William offered to give Harold
half the English kingdom with his daughter Adelaide when he,
William, succeeded Edward as king.[16]

William of Poitiers goes on to say that after the oath William
equipped the earl and his men splendidly for war and took
them on campaign against Conan fitzAlan, count of Brittany,
who had renounced his vassalage, was interfering in Maine and
being generally difficult.[17] William and Harold relieved Dol,
which was under siege by Conan; but the duke abandoned the
pursuit of the count because of the unknown terrain, the shortage of provisions and some other difficulties. (The archdeacon
possibly cut the campaign short in order to minimize Harold's
participation in it.) On their return to Rouen, William kept
Harold with him for a while and then sent him home laden

with gifts and with one of the two hostages in his hands, Harold's nephew (Hacon).

William of Poitiers's account is splendidly illustrated, expanded and modified on the Bayeux Tapestry,[18] which was probably designed in the 1070s and embroidered in England, probably at St Augustine's, Canterbury. Its patron would seem to have been the Conqueror's half-brother, Odo, Bishop of Bayeux, disgraced in 1082; and its purpose was not only to commemorate a great Norman achievement but also to stress the parts played in it by the bishop, then Earl of Kent, and Eustace Count of Boulogne, another companion of the Conqueror and a large landowner in England. Between William and Harold it is remarkably neutral in tone. The tapestry gives the fullest account of what happened to Harold between taking his leave of the king and his return some weeks later; but the pictures are not always easily decipherable and the legend is basic and sometimes unhelpful. The opening scene is of the king in his palace instructing the earl, who then rides with his thegns to his manor of Bosham, apparently doing some hunting and hawking en route. On arrival at Bosham, Harold and one of his company pray in the church before they all drink deep, and no doubt eat, in the manor hall. They embark in a single ship, probably towing a dinghy, Harold still carrying his hawk, others the hounds. (They were surely aiming at the Cotentin peninsula in Normandy, and the tapestry shows an uneventful channel crossing.[19] But, if so, they sailed badly off course, for they made a northerly landing in Ponthieu.) There Harold is arrested by the local count, Guy, as he wades ashore. He draws a knife but is overpowered. Guy then takes him to Beaurain in the extreme north of his county and holds him there. It was on the frontier with Eustace II's county of Boulogne; and Guy may have been demanding a ransom or some concession from Harold under threat of surrendering him to his old enemy of 1051. The count and the earl are shown having a parley, Guy seated on his throne and carrying an upright sword, Harold holding his unbelted sword in his left hand and apparently making submissive gestures.

Whatever Harold may have offered Guy, however, came to nothing because of the arrival of Duke William's men demanding the surrender of the earl to the duke under threat of military action. William had been informed of Harold's plight by one of his company who had escaped, and had acted with speed. He badly wanted to get his hands on the earl. Guy conducted Harold, once more carrying his hawk and riding with hounds, in person to the border town of Eu on the River Bresle. In the margin under Harold is a little picture of a naked man about to embrace a naked woman. This is the first of a series of three featuring a naked man; and although they may be a general reference to Harold's lechery, the precise meaning is unfathomable. William then takes him to his palace at Rouen, where the two confer in the great hall. This scene on the tapestry is 'explained' by three enigmatic pictures.[20] In the lower margin a naked man is wielding a tool and working on an oblong, probably wooden, object, perhaps a coffin. This may signify a man digging his own grave. In the main picture, Harold is gesturing with his left hand to the rear — perhaps to a bearded warrior who seems to be holding Harold's left hand, or possibly to the following scene. Here we have what the designer of the tapestry clearly considered an important event. Firmly located in the palace or at its gate, in a setting of architectural splendour, a woman, heavily robed, with only her face, hands and shoes disclosed, possibly a nun, is being molested by a clerk. Placing his left hand on his hip, he stretches out his right arm and is either touching her face or unveiling her. Then, in the lower margin, is a crouching naked man, his genitals emphasized, mirroring the gestures of the clerk. The legend in the upper margin is, 'ubi unus clericus et ÆLFGYVA', literally, 'where one clerk and Ælfgifu', a sentence which has often been completed but without improving our understanding of the scene. And this obviously improper event, despite sustained interest by historians, has never been satisfactorily explained. Harold had a sister named Ælfgifu, but it was a common name in aristocratic circles. The illustration would seem to commemorate a scandal that has left no other traces; and although the part it played in Harold's story cannot be imagined, it must have been important. It is just possible that it is an allusion to the Norman story of a projected marriage alliance between the Godwins and the duke.[21]

The tapestry then turns immediately to the Breton campaign and shows the duke and earl as brothers-in-arms and on excellent terms. They were in fact about the same age — approaching forty — with William probably a year or two younger than Harold. As they cross the treacherous River Couesnon, the boundary between Normandy and Brittany, Harold performs a feat of great strength and heroism. Beneath Mont-Saint-Michel, which is featured in the top border, Harold, on foot but still clutching his shield, drags two soldiers out of the quicksands. As these seem to be clean-shaven they may well have been Normans. According to the tapestry, the ducal army pursued Conan to Rennes and then Dinan, which fortress he surrendered to William. This episode closes with an impressive scene: 'William gave arms to Harold', presumably a knighting ceremony at the conclusion of a victorious campaign. The two figures, clad in chain mail and wearing swords, stand together in isolation. William is shown a little taller and stouter than Harold. The earl in his left hand holds a banner of command, which the duke may just have given him, while the duke with his left hand puts a helmet on Harold's head and with his right hand adjusts the straps on his hauberk. Harold has clearly become William's vassal. There seems to have been no precedent for this scene in earlier Canterbury manuscripts. The tapestry story has the two of them return to Bayeux, where Harold takes the oath to William.

There is a splendid depiction of the oath-taking ceremony. Apparently in the open, in the presence of William who sits on a throne and wields a sword, and two attendants holding spears, Harold stands bare-headed between two altars or reliquaries, one portable, with outstretched arms touching both. William and one of the armed attendants point to Harold. The legend fobs us off with the laconic 'where Harold took an oath to Duke William', although there is room for an explanatory phrase, such as 'de corona' (concerning the crown). Even the decorations in the margins seem studiously non-committal.

One later writer contributes an interesting detail. According to *Brevis Relatio de Guillelmo nobilissimo*, written by a monk of Battle Abbey between 1114 and 1120, Harold, 'as many say', took a triple oath to William on a reliquary called 'the bull's eye'.[22] This would seem to be the one illustrated on the tapestry over which Harold's left hand hovers, for in the middle of the lid is a protuberance of mushroom shape, with a mark in the centre of its head. In contrast, the reliquary Harold touches with his right hand has a lid with a cross at each end, and underneath, a stretcher for carrying it. In the so-called *Hyde Chronicle* the reliquary is also described as the phylactery of St Pancras, named the bull's eye because it has a large and most precious jewel in its midst.[23]

It will have been noticed that William of Poitiers and the tapestry differ on the location and the timing of the oath. And the uncertainty continues. Orderic Vitalis expressly corrected the archdeacon of Lisieux by placing it at Rouen,[24] and Guernes of Pont-Sainte-Maxence, in his life of St Thomas Becket written in 1172–4, designates the chamber of the favourite ducal hunting lodge at Bur-le-Roi, near Bayeux, as the place where Harold, after being affianced to William's daughter, Rainild

(?*recte* Adelaide), who died young, pledges the loyalty of the English army to William.[25]

The tapestry concludes its depiction of Harold's visit to the continent with the earl's return to the royal court. The homecomer is shown making supplicatory gestures to Edward who, sitting on a bench, points a finger at him. An axeman standing behind the earl also points to him and moreover seems to threaten him with the blade of his weapon, while another axeman, standing behind Edward, points to the king, but with his blade averted. As usual there is no marginal explanation; but it would seem that Harold is being admonished.

After the Norman Conquest English authors rewrote this whole episode. About 1112, Eadmer, the Canterbury monk of English birth and lineage, in his *Historia Novorum in Anglia* (history of recent events in England), claimed that the expedition was Harold's idea, that he insisted on going against Edward's wishes and despite his forebodings, in order to secure the release of the hostages taken from the family, and that William took advantage of Harold's recklessness.[26] William tells Harold that Edward, when a boy in exile in Normandy (1016–1041), had promised him that if ever he obtained the English throne he would make him his successor by hereditary right; and William now wishes the earl to help him achieve this. He wants him to put Dover Castle with its water well at the duke's disposal, to hand over at a convenient time his sister, whom the duke will marry to one of his chief men, and Harold himself to marry William's daughter. In return the duke will release Harold's nephew then and there, and Harold's brother when he, William, eventually comes to reign in England. Also, when king through Harold's help, he will grant the earl all his reasonable requests. Eadmer insists that Harold perceived all the dangers latent in such a compact, but realized that he was trapped. So he agreed. Whereupon William assembled holy relics upon which Harold took the required oath.

The earl, Eadmer continues, then returned to England with his nephew, only to be reminded by the king that his warnings had been justified, and that, by disregarding them, Harold had got them all into a mess. Harold, however, neglected his obligations to the duke and, when William complained, Harold replied that his sister had died, but William could have her corpse if he wished; that he had fulfilled his undertaking re Dover, although he did not know to whom he had surrendered it; that, as regards the kingdom, how could he have given it away, or promised it, before he had actually possessed it?; and, lastly, that he could not possibly bring in a foreign woman as queen without the consent of the English nobles. These answers, which probably owe more to Eadmer than to Harold, are *ben trovato* and cheeky. Although there are reticences here, Eadmer makes a good point. Harold bowed to *force majeure*.

The Norman story is also revised, more briefly than by Eadmer, by William of Malmesbury, writing some time after 1125.[27] He picks up and develops the sporting aspect of the trip indicated by the tapestry and gives a new reason for Harold's appearance in Ponthieu and Normandy. Harold and his party had embarked at Bosham on a fishing boat purely for recreation, and had been pushed across the channel by a sudden storm. When captured and imprisoned by Count Guy, Harold bribes a man with enormous promises to go to William of Normandy and inform him of the disaster and also to explain (falsely) that the earl had been on his way to the duke, sent by King Edward. When released by William's efforts, Harold was so grateful and so impressed by William's subsequent kindnesses that of his own accord he promised to surrender to him Dover Castle immediately and the kingdom itself after Edward's death.

In Scandinavia another version was current. One summer Harold, when sailing for Wales, was diverted by bad weather to Normandy. And, desiring to marry the duke's daughter, he stayed there until the following spring (*King Harald's Saga*, cap. 76).

As the story develops, contradictions and reassessments appear. And one key matter, why Harold made the journey, remains uncertain. It is easy to suggest reasons which fall far outside the Norman case. For example, at the end of 1063 Edward's nephew, Walter count of Mantes, had been defeated and imprisoned by William. The fate of this prince, who had a better hereditary claim to the English throne than William, could have been of interest to Edward and Harold. The one thing that is absolutely clear is that the Norman case is based on the premise that Edward, from beginning to end, wanted William to succeed him on the English throne, and took all the steps he could to bring it about. If it then be accepted that in 1064–5 Edward sent Harold to the duke to confirm the bequest, all that follows, the oath and the promises, is understandable. There are, however, a number of caveats. There is no good evidence that Edward ever or consistently regarded William as his heir.

Wealthy men without close blood heirs are notoriously fickle. Certainly since 1052 Edward had been looking elsewhere, and there is nothing to show that he and William had been in recent contact.[28] Harold's foreign trip in 1064/5, shown on the tapestry as a pleasure jaunt, may or may not have been aimed at Rouen, but that it landed up in the mouth of the Somme seems more than careless. Then it would seem unlikely that the Godwins would have favoured such a royal policy. A 'natural' heir, Edgar Atheling, was after all at the royal court. Indeed, as future events were to show, there was no party in England which favoured William's cause.

It must, however, be accepted that whatever the circumstances may have been, Harold fell into William's grasp and took an oath of some sort. Here there seem to be fewer problems. The duke held Harold's nephew and brother hostage; he had freed the earl from imprisonment by Guy of Ponthieu; and there was no way in which Harold could escape from William, except by agreeing to his demands. We can accept that he took an oath of fealty to William, perhaps did homage, and probably agreed that he would support and advance the duke's claim to the English throne. There could also have been some more specific undertakings. But William of Poitiers is probably pushing it too hard when claiming that Harold offered these of his own free will. Eadmer is more convincing. Harold bowed to *force majeure*, and could surely have argued in any tribunal that promises extorted under duress were invalid. It is by no means unlikely also that the crafty earl, who 'usually passed with watchful mockery through all ambushes unscathed',[29] submitted without any intention of limiting his options or of observing the terms. Which is what happened.

In the meantime some of the leading actors in these events were taking care of their afterlife. In England the king and queen made religious foundations. The tenth-century reformation of the English church, patronized by King Edgar (959–75), which had been aimed primarily at the reimposition of the Rule of St Benedict on secularized monasteries, had come to a sudden end with the viking invasions in Æthelred's reign. Earl Æthelmaer, Godwin's probable grandfather, had been a patron of Ælfric the Homilist and had founded the abbeys of Cerne in Dorset and Eynsham in Oxfordshire at the beginning of the eleventh century. But neither the king nor his Danish successors had been much concerned with the state of the church or had founded a monastery. To what extent the newly christianized Danes held to their old heathen ways is unclear. King Cnut certainly tried with some success to be a Christian king, issuing an ecclesiastical as well as a secular code of laws and paying a visit to the pope at Rome; and it was, perhaps, his early death which prevented his founding or greatly enriching some religious body. But his great servant, Earl Godwin, seems in his lifetime to have evinced no Christian piety. Indeed, he was considered a despoiler of the church. This, however, may be unduly harsh, for there is evidence that he refounded the minster at Dover as a college of secular canons and moved it from its original site on the shore to the shelter of the Iron Age hill fort on the cliff top.[30]

In Edward's reign, however, in a time of peace and prosperity, there was a change in fashion. Odda of Deerhurst, perhaps a relation of the king, who was appointed earl over the western shires during the Godwins' exile, built a chapel at Deerhurst which still stands, and was a patron of Pershore Abbey where he became a monk and died in 1056. The Worcester chronicle calls him 'a lover of churches'.[31] The king himself, who for most of his life exhibited little of those qualities which earned him his posthumous canonization, made towards the end of his life the grandest foundation, the rebuilding of Westminster Abbey, which is carefully described in *Vita* and shown on the Bayeux Tapestry.[32] Edith's foundation, according to *Vita*, the rebuilding in stone of Wilton Abbey, the house where she was educated, was a more modest undertaking.[33] But from an Evesham Abbey source we learn that the king and queen collaborated in searching for relics and that Edith was the more predatory.[34] The story goes that once, before Christmas, when the royal court was to meet as usual at Gloucester, they ordered several of the neighbouring monasteries to send their reliquaries there; and it was feared at Evesham that the queen intended making a selection for Wilton. Evesham safeguarded itself by sending, instead of the relics of St Egwin, its greatest patron, those of St Odulf; and this saint stoutly defended his church. On the day after Christmas, when a goldsmith opened the shrines for Edith's inspection and he came to the Evesham chest and put in his hand, Edith was suddenly struck blind. In her distress she ordered the smith to desist and promised God she would never again do an injury to the saints if through the merits of St Odulf she could recover her sight; and she also bestowed a special pall on the shrine she had violated. Where-upon her sight was restored.

The rebuilding of Wilton was hindered by a fire which broke out in the town and destroyed all those things that Edith had assembled for the dedication of the church. But, apparently before the autumn of 1065, it was dedicated by Bishop Herman of Ramsbury, an occasion celebrated by the Godwins' encomi-ast with a poem, a 'metaphorical epithalamium', which con-cluded with a paraphrase of Psalm 83 (Vulgate). Wilton, 'this bride of God', will give birth to a numerous progeny:

> *Nor in slow time do you produce slow birth*
> *By ordered lapse of those long, lazy months:*
> *Loved by your spouse for your fecundity*
> *Each day you celebrate the many births.*

And father God will rain manna from Heaven on these nurselings.[35] The childless Edith was in compensation to have many spiritual daughters. And her husband the king, in his last illness, granted two hides of land in Amesbury to the abbess.[36]

The nunnery, which Edith also enriched, was frequented by the hagiographer, Goscelin of Saint-Bertin, a possible author of *Vita*, who loved one of the nuns, Eve, the daughter of a Dane and a Lotharingian woman. He was with Eve and her mother at the banquet after the dedication in 1065, when he sent the girl a fish.[37] And in his *Vita S. Kenelmi*, Goscelin claimed that the 'most learned Queen Edith' had given him some informa-tion about this most obscure early ninth-century Mercian prince whose shrine was at Winchcombe.[38] Wilton seems, indeed, to have been a cultured establishment, with its chaplains some-times recruited from Germany. Harold's daughter, Gunhild, and Malcolm Canmore's daughter, Edith, who was to marry King Henry I, were educated there; and one of its nuns, Muriel, was a well-known poet. It was a rich, aristocratic and not too strict society. Nevertheless, Edith was remembered more as a despoiler than as an enricher of the English church.[39]

Harold founded a house of secular canons at Waltham in Essex before 1060. According to the twelfth-century history of its foundation,[40] Waltham (as its name shows) was a hunting lodge on the lands of Tovi the Proud, an important servant of King Cnut, his standard bearer and staller, at whose marriage feast on 8 June 1042 King Harthacnut had fallen dead. When a black stone crucifix (the Holy Cross) was discovered on Tovi's manor of Montacute in Somerset, he moved it to Waltham where he created a village with 66 men and rebuilt the church to be served by two priests. King Edward took Waltham from Tovi's son and transferred it to Harold, who transformed the church, its buildings (although 'a freakish, bizarre plan') and its constitution, on Lotharingian lines.[41] According to the tradition preserved at Waltham, the reform was associated with a severe illness, described as 'paralysis', which Harold suffered. The emperor of Germany, probably Henry III (1039–56), sent master Adelard, a native of Liège (now in Belgium), educated at Utrecht (now in Holland), to cure him. And Adelard advised the earl to seek a cure at the Holy Cross of Waltham. In gratitude for his cure there, Harold transformed the existing church. He appointed a dean, Wulfwig, and twelve canons (the apostolic number) including Adelard and men chosen from the principal communities in England. Adelard and Wulfwig devised the rule under which the canons were to live and advised Harold generally on the society's requirements. Adelard had a son, master Peter, who taught at Waltham, and among his pupils was the historian of the church.

Harold lavished his wealth on this enterprise. And, as the college was in touch with Edith Swan-neck in 1066, it may be that she, a Norfolk woman, was also involved. The revenues alloted to the canons (their prebends) were most generous; the supplements to their diet on special occasions (the pittances) were extravagant; and the twelfth-century canon who wrote an account of the foundation describes lovingly the excellent construction of the building and its fine pavement, the splendour of the interior decorations, the richness of its furnishings and ornaments, its vestments and service books. Gold and silver, but above all gold, were everywhere. Some of the silver vases had been made for Tovi's wife, Gytha, by the leading London goldsmith, Theodoric, probably Edward's well known smith and moneyer, a German.[42] Gold thread and pearls adorned the vestments. The gold used in the decoration of one chasuble, known as 'The Lord said unto me', weighed 26 marks, that is to say over 17 pounds. This vestment King William Rufus (1087–1100) took away, together with some other treasures, and presented to two churches at Caen, perhaps his parents' two abbeys. The altar was of marble, supported in front by golden statues of the twelve apostles and behind by golden lions. Harold also provided sixty holy relics which master Adelard listed in the chapter book. Some were of English origin: two came from Ely and rather more from the West Country. Most of the rest he had probably collected on his travels abroad. One group had a Roman, perhaps papal, origin. The others mostly originated in Flanders, Germany and northern France: from St-Armand in Ghent and St-Ghislain near Mons in Flanders, St-Riquier in Ponthieu, Cologne in Germany, and Noyon, Rheims and Metz in France. The second largest gift of relics came from an even greater traveller, Bishop Ealdred, presumably because of his friendship with Harold.[43]

Harold invited to the dedication of the church, probably in 1060 on 3 May (the feast of the Invention of the Holy Cross), the king and queen and the leading men of the kingdom. The consecrator was Archbishop Cynsige of York, 'because Canterbury was vacant'. If Stigand, who was in possession of Canterbury and holding it in plurality with Winchester, was in fact available and excluded, Harold must have regarded his position as uncanonical. Edward is said to have remained at Waltham for a week and to have confirmed Harold's gifts both verbally and by a charter written in letters of gold, signed by a golden cross from his own hand. Although the authenticity of an elaborate royal charter in favour of Harold and Waltham and with a very large witness list, dated 1062, has been doubted, it has also been strongly supported.[44] The college was refounded as an Augustinian priory in 1177, when the canon who had described its glories was expelled, and as an abbey in 1184. It may well have been Harold's final resting place.

Harold's younger brothers were less ostentatious in their benefactions to the church. Tostig and his wife Judith of Flanders were benefactors of Durham.[45] Judith, a great admirer of St Cuthbert, gave the church many ornaments, and promised even more, together with lands, if she could enter the church and pay homage to the saint at his tomb. As no woman was allowed to enter the cathedral or its cemetery, Judith sent one of her maids, who volunteered, to test the defences. And when the girl put a foot inside the cemetery she was instantly repelled by a violent blast of air and died in torment shortly after she returned home. Judith, terrified by the girl's fate, in expiation for the crime gave the church a crucifix, statues of the Virgin Mary and St John the Evangelist, both clad in gold and silver and specially commissioned by the earl and countess, as well as many other ornaments.

Harold and Tostig's younger brothers were not yet of an age to be concerned with such matters. Their youngest sister Gunhild, however, had a religious vocation.[46]

On the other side of the channel, William of Normandy and his Flemish wife Matilda, when they made their peace with the pope in 1059 for their uncanonical and prohibited marriage, undertook each to found a convent. This they did at Caen. And to the nunnery, Holy Trinity, they 'sacrificed' a daughter, Cecily, who rose to be abbess. Thus all these ambitious rulers were striving to get God on their side through the mediation of their religious foundations, their national churches, and the pope.

Notes

1. *Vita*, pp. 58–9.
2. Cf. *ASC* 'D', *s.a.* 1057.
3. Lloyd, *History*, ii. 357 ff. for Gruffydd.
4. *ASC* 'C', cf. 'D', *s.a.* 1056.
5. *ASC* 'D', *s.a.* 1058.
6. Lloyd, 'Wales and the coming of the Normans, 1039–93', *Transactions of the Hon. Soc. of Cymmrodorion* (1899–1900), pp. 134–8; *History*, ii, 369–73.
7. *Vita*, pp. 86–7; *ASC* 'D', *s.a.* 1063; John of Worcester, ii. 592–3.
8. Giraldus Cambrensis, *Descriptio Kambriae*, in *Opera Omnia*, ed. J.F. Dimock (Rolls ser., 1868), vi. 217.
9. John of Salisbury, *Johannis Saresbiriensis episcopi Carnotensis Policraticus*, ed. C.C.J. Webb (1909), VI, vi, ii. 19–20.
10. Gaimar, v. 5084.
11. *GG*, i, 43, ed. Chibnall, pp. 74–5. K.S.B. Keats-Rohan, 'William I and the Breton contingent in the non-Norman Conquest, 1060–1087', *ANS*, xiii (1991), 164, strongly supports 1064.
12. Körner, pp. 26–7, 76–138.
13. *Carmen*, vv. 231–4, 239–42, 290–9.
14. Above, p. 77; cf. below, p. 117.
15. *GG*, i. 41–6, ed. Chibnall, pp. 68–79.
16. *GG*, ii. 32, ed. Chibnall, pp. 136–7; *GND*, ii. 160–2; OV, ii. 136–7, cf. iii. 114–15. For Adelaide see Barlow, *William Rufus*, appendix A.
17. *GG*, i. 43–5, ed. Chibnall, pp. 70–7.
18. *BT*, pl. 1–31; Barlow, *Carmen*, pp. lviii–lx. A.J. Taylor, 'Belrem', *ANS*, xiv (1992), 1–23.
19. It was normal practice to cross the channel by the shortest sea route: see map 2, M. Gardiner, 'Shipping and trade between England and the Continent during the eleventh century', *ANS*, xxii (2000), p. 77.
20. *BT*, pl. 17–19. Taylor, 'Belrem', p. 12. C. Hart, 'The Bayeux Tapestry and schools of illumination at Canterbury', *ANS*, xxii (2000),

117–68, is of no help here. Either there were no such obscene pictures in earlier Canterbury mss, or he did not wish to show them.

21. Walker, p. 226, n. 9.

22. Ed. Elisabeth M.C. van Houts, *Camden Miscellany*, xxxiv, Camden 5th ser. x (1997), 1–48, at p. 28.

23. *Chronica monasterii de Hida* in *Liber monasterii de Hyda*, ed. E. Edwards (Rolls ser. 1866), 283–321, at p. 290. An interesting paper on the bull's eye and the blinding of Harold is D. Bernstein, 'The blinding of Harold and the meaning of the Bayeux Tapestry', *ANS*, v (1983), 40–64. Hart (as above, n. 20) in a note on the altars, which he shows in fig. 28, cf. 6, merely comments that modern commentators consider that the 'bull's eye' represents the Host (i.e. the consecrated bread of the Mass).

24. OV, ii. 134–5. The author of the thirteenth-century legendary history of Harold claims that he had been shown a withered oak near Rouen under which Harold had taken the oath: *Vita Haroldi*, ed. W. de Gray Birch (1885), p. 50.

25. Guernes, vv. 5096–5100. For William's daughters, see Barlow, *William Rufus* (1983), appendix A.

26. *Eadmeri Historia Novorum in Anglia*, ed. M. Rule (Rolls ser. 1884), pp. 6–8. On occasion Eadmer utilized Æthelric II, formerly monk of Christ Church, Canterbury, and bishop of Selsey, as a source.

27. *GR*, i. 279–80. Freeman, *FNC*, iii, 688–9, accepted William's view enthusiastically and expanded it by making Wulfnoth and Hacon Harold's companions. The nephew returned with him, but he left his brother behind as a hostage.

28. Barlow, *Edward*, ch. X.

29. *Vita*, pp. 52–3.

30. *FNC*, ii, app. note E. 'The alleged spoliation of the church by Godwine and Harold'; A. Williams, 'The estates of Harold Godwineson', *ANS*, iii (1981), 181–4, 'Thegnly piety and ecclesiastical patronage in the late Old English Kingdom', *ANS*, xxiv (2002), 8. See also above, p. 91, n. 18.

31. *ASC, s.a.* 1051, 1056; Ann Williams, *Land, Power and Politics: the family and career of Odda of Deerhurst*, The Deerhurst lecture, 1991 (Deerhurst 1993), 'Thegnly piety and ecclesiastical patronage', *ANS*, xxiv (2002), 15–17.

32. *Vita*, pp. 66–71, 110–15; *BT*, pl. 32.

33. *Vita*, pp. 70–5.
34. 'Translation and Miracles of S. Odulph', *Chronicon abbatiae de Evesham*, ed. W.D. Macray (Rolls ser., 1863), pp. 317–18.
35. *Vita*, pp. 72–5.
36. *DB*, i. 64v.
37. Barlow, *Vita*, pp. 138–9.
38. *Vita S. Kenelmi, regis et martyris* (BHL, no. 4641 n.), ed. R.C. Love, *Three Eleventh-Century Anglo-Latin Saints' Lives* (1996), Oxford University Press, Oxford, p. 52.
39. Stafford, pp. 145–6.
40. *The Foundation of Waltham Abbey. The Tract 'De Inventione Sanctae Crucis nostrae in Monte Acuto et de ductione eiusdem apud Waltham'*, ed. W. Stubbs (Oxford, 1861); a new edn is by M. Chibnall (OMT, 1994). *Vita Haroldi*, trans. Swanton, pp. 6–9.
41. Dinah Dean, *The Five Churches of Waltham Abbey, Essex* (undated pamphlet); Richard Plant, 'English Romanesque and the empire', *ANS*, xxiv (2002), 182, 'Ecclesiastical Architecture *c*. 1056 to *c*. 1200', *A Companion to the Anglo-Norman World*, ed. C. Harper-Bill and E. van Houts (2003), p. 217; Ann Williams, 'Thegnly piety and ecclesiastical patronage', *ANS*, xxiv (2002), 14–19.
42. For Theodoric, see Stafford, pp. 115–16.
43. *The Foundation*, pp. 20–1; Walker, pp. 72–3; Walcot, 'Inventory of Waltham, Holy Cross', *Trans. Essex Arch. Soc.*, v (1873), 257–64, at p. 261.
44. Sawyer, no. 1036; S. Keynes, 'Regenbald the Chancellor (*sic*)', *ANS*, x (1998), 201–3, and Stafford, p. 108, however, are inclined to accept it.
45. See above, p. 92, n. 45.
46. See below, pp. 167–8.

chapter 6

HAROLD'S TRIUMPH, 1065–1066

The first glimpse we have of Harold after his return from Normandy is the notice in the chronicle under 1065 that he had invaded south Wales.[1] The twelfth-century life of St Gwynllyw may throw some light on this.[2] It tells how some English merchants trading to the mouth of the Usk [Newport] refused to pay the customary toll, whereupon Rhiryd, son of Ifor and grandson of King Gruffydd, cut their anchor away and offered it at the shrine of the saint at Newport. The merchants complained to Harold, who assembled an army and invaded and ravaged Glamorgan as far as the Usk. Some of his troops violated the saint's church, but failed to find the anchor. When they began to cut up the cheeses they found there, these started to bleed, which so terrified the soldiers that they ceased to loot and Harold made an offering at the altar.

More certainly Harold ordered some buildings to be constructed at Portskewitt a few miles south-west of Chepstow, in what is now Monmouthshire, presumably to provide the merchants with a safer base than Newport. And he was minded to invite King Edward there to hunt. This would probably have been in late summer, for the fat season, 'grease time', for red deer stags opened on 1 August and closed on 14 September. Portskewitt, however, was in Gwent and subject to the Welsh prince Caradog ap Gruffydd ap Rhydderch, who ruled over Gwynllwg and Upper Gwent. And on 24 August Caradog raided the site, killed all the workmen and took all the goods assembled there. Edward went hunting with Tostig in Wiltshire instead.

This minor setback for the house of Godwin was followed by a major disaster, a rebellion against Tostig.[3] The insurrection started, according to John of Worcester, on 3 October, when three otherwise unknown Yorkshire thegns, Gamelbearn, Dunstan son of Æthelnoth and Glonieorn son of Heardwulf, went with 200 armed men to York, where they seized two of Tostig's house-carls, Amund and Ravenswart, whom they killed outside the city walls. They then broke open his treasury and armoury and looted his goods. They also the following day slaughtered more than 200 of Tostig's men south of the city. This sparked off a general uprising involving, according to the chronicle, all the thegns of Yorkshire. These declared Tostig an outlaw and sent for Morcar, the younger brother of Earl Edwin of Mercia, whom they elected earl. According to *Vita*, there was ill will from long-standing rivalry between the Mercian pair and Tostig,[4] presumably because of their contests over earldoms. And Morcar led them, together with insurgents from Nottinghamshire, Derbyshire and Lincolnshire, south to Northampton, where they were joined by Edwin and some Welsh troops. Harold met the rebels at Northampton and negotiated. They asked him to persuade the king to give them Morcar as earl; and, while Harold went on this errand, they devastated the area. They killed many people and captured many hundreds more, and burned houses and corn. Their human captives and the thousands of cattle they seized they took back with them when they returned north. *Vita* claims that they slaughtered without trial anyone who had any connection with Tostig in York and Lincoln and throughout the earldom, and makes them advance as far south as Oxford. And a poem which may refer to this phase concludes: 'Thus madness on ungrateful lands will heap / the bounty looted in the hostile towns.'[5]

It was at Oxford that the king through messengers ordered them to stop ravaging and take their grievances to law. He would see that they received right and justice for every injury they could prove. But they demanded, as a first condition, the deposition and exile of Tostig. This was on 28 October, according to Chronicle 'C'. Edward held a great council at Britford, near Salisbury, but found little support for Tostig among the magnates. Some accused the earl of cruelty, rapacity and injustice. Some suspected Harold as being the instigator of the rebellion; and Tostig charged him with this before the assembly — a charge which Harold denied on oath. In the end Edward decided to crush the insurrection by force and summoned an army. But the response was poor; and finally, just before Christmas 1065, the king had to accept defeat. Tostig and Judith and their children and some of their thegns left for Flanders, where Count Baldwin received them warmly. He put the exile in charge of Saint-Omer, apparently as assistant to, or replacement for, the existing castellan, Lambert, or his son Wulfric Rabel.[6]

All the sources agree that the basic cause of the insurrection was Tostig's strong and oppressive government. Anglo-Saxon Chronicle 'C' blames Tostig for robbing God and depriving men less powerful than himself of life and law.

An example of Tostig's enforcement of law and order, provided by a Durham miracle story,[7] is largely to the earl's credit. A notorious malefactor, Aldan-hamal, arrested about 1060 on suspicion of theft, robbery, murder and arson, was condemned to death; and all attempts by kinsmen and friends to bribe Tostig to release him were fruitless. But while the man was in fetters in prison at Durham awaiting execution, he repented of his crimes and promised St Cuthbert that if he could go free he would fully atone for them. St Cuthbert heard his prayers, struck off his fetters and allowed him to escape into the cathedral church. Tostig's guards, under his thegn Barcwith, had no respect for the right of sanctuary, for, they thought, it would allow all thieves, robbers and murderers to laugh in their faces. So they went in pursuit of Aldan-hamal, and were preparing to break into the church, which had been barred against them, when God struck Barcwith down, and within an hour or two he died, raving mad. Tostig, terrified by Barcwith's fate, pardoned the criminal, and later took him into his favour. The guards made such large expiatory offerings on the saint's tomb that a cross and a New Testament were adorned with gold and silver and jewels in order to provide memorials of this miraculous event which would serve as a warning to others.

For the revolt against Tostig in 1065 John of Worcester identifies two immediate grievances;[8] firstly, the slaughter of three noble Northumbrian thegns, Gospatric killed at the royal court on Queen Edith's orders for Tostig's sake on 28 December 1064 and Gamal son of Orm and Ulf son of Godwin, both of whom Tostig had treacherously killed in his own chamber at York in the previous year, although they were protected by a pledge of peace;[9] and, secondly, an enormous tax which he had wrongfully imposed on Northumbria. It was presumably the tax rather than the 'murder' of a few notables which caused such widespread discontent. But if Tostig had indeed increased the burden of geld, the national land tax, either by changing assessments or by increasing the efficiency of the collection, perhaps by extending it to hitherto exempt areas, it must have been with the consent of the king. And it may be significant that Edward, when negotiating at Northampton, renewed for the province the law of King Cnut.[10] Whether Tostig was a firm ruler of a lawless province or a lawless tyrant depends on the point of view. His accusation that Harold had instigated the trouble is at first sight surprising and is difficult to judge. Both versions of *The Anglo-Saxon Chronicle* follow Caradog's

attack on Portskewitt immediately with the Northumbrian rebellion; and in version 'D', with reference to Portskewitt are
the dark words: 'We do not know who first suggested this
conspiracy.' It could be implied that Edwin Earl of Mercia, or
even Tostig, had intrigued with the Welshman to injure Harold.
To which he replied in kind.

Vita throughout, and particularly in three poems, regards
the quarrel between Harold and Tostig as responsible for the
collapse of the family's fortunes. The only ambiguity is where
lay the blame. The verses after chapter 5, which deals with
England at peace and prosperous under the rule of Godwin's
sons, especially Harold and Tostig, are devoted entirely to the
horrors that have ensued from family feuds.[11] From classical
mythology are cited the warring sons of Oedipus, the twins
Eteocles and Polynices,[12] and the sons of Pelops, Atreus and
Thyestes, and from the Bible, Cain and Abel, the sons of Adam
and Eve. Heaven preserve England from such discord! The
third poem, which prefaces Book II of *Vita* and changes the
subject from the Godwins to Edward's claims to sanctity,
laments that these dire precedents have been followed. As a
result of the quarrel between Harold and Tostig both are dead
and the chaos of hell has arrived. In this poem the two brothers
incur equal blame: 'Alas these brothers' hearts too hard!'[13]

The first poem on the subject, that which follows the mostly
lost chapter 2 devoted to Godwin's children, is rather different.[14] Concerned entirely with discord within Godwin's family,
the actors in the drama are disguised in a riddle. Since one
individual or party is described as good, the other as evil, the
poet is being discreet. He has to consider the feelings of his
patron, the queen, the sister of the antagonists. He likens
Godwin to the spring in Paradise from which four rivers sprang.
The origin of this conceit is the Book of Genesis in the Bible
(ii. 10–14) where, in the Creation story, God planted the garden
of Eden in which Adam and Eve were to live; and a river went

out to water the garden, and from thence it parted and became four heads. But the biblical imagery is of no further help. Whereas in Genesis the four rivers go out to water four different regions of the earth, in *Vita*, after the dissimilarity of the four is stressed, they are apparently grouped into two pairs (*pars haec, pars illa*). A further complication is that the only child named is Edith, who heads the list. But as she is described not as a river but as a gem on the kingdom's breast, her appearance seems to be either an irrelevance or an awkward intrusion. Most likely, therefore, the four are those sons of Godwin who are named in the narrative and were doubtless all discussed in chapter 2, that is to say, Harold, Tostig, Gyrth and Leofwine. And if these have to be paired, it would seem that Leofwine usually went with Harold, Gyrth with Tostig.

In seven lines the poet contrasts the behaviour of the two parts. One rises to the sky, clings to things above, and raises its offspring in a nest in a high tree. The other part, a hostile devourer, swims across seeking the depths. Doing damage to its own stock and hanging by its beak, it holds on to the treetrunk from which it was born, until, at a fixed time of its life, the breath of life creates an animal from an inanimate mother. When released from her, it devotes itself to its own plunderings. If each part represents two rivers, that is to say two sons, it is awkward that the parts are represented by one creature. One investigator of this problem, however, Rhona Beare, who has given much attention to the poem,[15] identifies both parts as birds, the first as the swift or swallow, the second as the mythical barnacle-goose. This may well be so; but these identifications provide little, if any, help to naming the man or men thus disguised.

Nor are the two easily recognizable from the mysterious descriptions of their behaviour. Beare thinks that the good swallow is Harold, the bad goose Tostig. But the opposite seems more likely. The encomiast usually devotes more space to Tostig than to Harold, and in his account of the 1065 rebellion gives a clear indication that he (and presumably Edith) thought that Harold was involved in the revolt: Harold rebutted the charge on oath — but, alas, he was too free with his oaths. As for the clues in the poem, although Harold flew high when he ascended the throne and was certainly up to a point the most successful of the four brothers, the reference to his offspring being reared in a nest at the top of a tree rings no bell. His children from Edith Swan-neck would not seem to be out of 'the top drawer', whereas Tostig's wife was the half-sister of Baldwin V, the reigning count of Flanders. Moreover, the poem ends with the disasters which would occur if evil malice should break the concord by provoking whirlwinds. Now the encomiast, when describing the revolt against Tostig in 1065, has the rebels gather together 'like a whirlwind or tempest'.[16] It is likely, therefore, that in the poem he was alluding to that same event, and when he mentions the tall cedar which would be uprooted and crash down with all the precious things it was keeping warm in its bosom, presumably chicks in the nests,[17] he was referring to the exile of Tostig and Judith and their family as a result of the insurrection. If so, Harold is the devouring monster. His success was at the expense of others, especially Tostig.

A subsidiary theme in *Vita* is that a treaty or compact was broken when the brothers quarrelled.[18] This would presumably have been a Godwinist plan, devised by Queen Edith, for which *Vita* itself was originally a fore-runner or justification. But what that scheme was is uncertain. Most likely Edith, like many strong women of the period, envisaged herself as remaining in power after the death of her husband and, like Edward, using her brothers as her agents. *Vita* seems to suppose that Harold had a long-standing ambition to succeed Edward and moved remorselessly to remove competitors. As Alfred Lord Tennyson put in Tostig's mouth before the battle of Stamford Bridge in 1066,

Thou hast no passion for the house of Godwin —
Thou hast but cared to make thyself a king.[19]

There is, however, little support for this outside *Vita* and the blackguarding Norman writers. English authors generally regarded him favourably. For example, Orderic Vitalis considered him 'A courageous and honourable (*probus*) man, strong and handsome, a witty speaker and affable to his supporters'.[20] A more charitable view of the earl of Wessex in the last years of Edward's reign would be that he was an opportunist, taking advantage of such chances as came his way. The substitution of Morcar for Tostig in Northumbria greatly enhanced the Mercian family's position. But Harold seems never to have been on bad terms with that dynasty. And in 1065 he could have considered the support of the Mercians essential for his plans, all the more if he distrusted Tostig. Certainly Tostig went into exile with a burning grievance against Harold, and in the following year did not hesitate to harm him. But if there was a general feeling among the English nobility that Tostig had governed badly and deserved his fate, it is difficult to see what Harold could have done to help his brother, even had he wanted to. He had tried to negotiate and had failed.

Vita states that Edward never recovered from the shock he suffered from his failure to save Tostig.[21] But there is no evidence for Edward's immediate decline in health. On Domesday Book evidence a legal judgment was to have been enforced in the royal court at Christmas.[22] And on Christmas Day Edward carried out his usual ceremonial duties. However, on the next day, 26 December, he had to retire to his bedchamber and was unable to attend the consecration of his new church at Westminster on 28 December. He died a week later, on 4 or 5

January, apparently from a stroke, and was buried in his abbey on the sixth, the feast of the Epiphany, the last important church festival before Easter. A generation later, Godfrey of Cambrai, prior of St Swithun's, Winchester, produced an unqualified, if a little colourless, tribute in his series of historical epigrams:[23]

Edward, powerful in his probity, revered for his goodness,
And governing both himself and his men, was a most illustrious king.
Fair of face and long in body,
His beauty was surpassed by the rectitude of his behaviour.
He had great wealth, but did not allow its abuse.
A rich man to others, he was a pauper to himself.
He confronted his enemies not with war but with peace:
And no one thought to violate his peace.
The entrance of Janus had given back five days of the year
When the king, leaving the temples of his flesh, expired.

On the same holy day that Edward was buried, Harold was consecrated as his successor. Although the coronation may have been simply opportunist, it must have had a background. Its antecedents, however, are purely conjectural. The paragraph in *Vita* about how Harold carefully studied, not only through servants but in person, the characters, policies and powers of the princes of Gaul in order to gauge what use they could be to him in the furtherance of any business of his,[24] could be understood as meaning he went looking for supporters for his claim to be Edward's heir. As the senior brother-in-law of the childless monarch and for long his coadjutor, he had a plausible case. But *Vita* gives the impression that the royal court preferred Tostig to Harold, although it would seem unlikely that Edward and Edith could seriously have imagined that Tostig could ever become king. None of the sources mentions here the one available male descendant of King Æthelred, Edgar Atheling, whose father, Edward 'the Exile', King Edward's half-nephew, had been enticed from Hungary in 1057, apparently to be adopted as heir and, aged about fourteen, was seemingly living at the royal court. The one recent precedent for a child king, Edward the Martyr, Æthelred's half-brother and predecessor, murdered in 978, was not encouraging. Edgar Atheling was not the son of a king. But he was the only 'legitimate' claimant and, after Harold's death at Hastings, was elected king by those notables who were in the city of London, including, according to Chronicle 'D', Archbishop Ealdred of York and Earls Edwin and Morcar, although, prudently, there was no hasty coronation.[25] As for William of Normandy and Swegen of Denmark, foreign rulers who had tenuous 'hereditary' claims, there is no evidence that either had even an active supporter in England, let alone a party. The throne was obviously there for the taking. Harold must have acquired supporters before Christmas 1066; and at some point he obtained large estates in Mercia, evidence for a compact between the two families.[26] He also lost no time after his coronation in marrying Edwin and Morcar's sister, the widow since 1063 of Gruffydd of Wales, a victim of Harold and Tostig's invasion.

The royal court at Westminster must have been exceptionally crowded at Christmas 1065, for the abbey church was dedicated, in the king's unavoidable absence, on 28 December. As, however, no royal charters are extant from this period, we have no lists of suitors. There is a dramatic description in *Vita* of Edward's last hours, with Edith warming her husband's feet in her lap, and Earl Harold, Robert fitzWimarch (Edward's kinsman and steward) and Archbishop Stigand of Canterbury in attendance.[27] The dying king's vision of the green tree, with the prophecy that within a year and a day of his death God would punish the kingdom for its sins by delivering it into the hands of its enemy, so that devils would go through the land with fire and sword and the havoc of war, was heard with horror by those present, with only the archbishop keeping his head. The encomiast also reports Edward's last words to those around him. To Edith he said: 'May God be gracious to this my wife for the zealous solicitude of her service; for certainly she has served me devotedly and always stood close by my side like a beloved daughter. May the forgiving God grant her the reward of eternal happiness.' Then, stretching out his hand to his 'tutor' (*nutricius*), her brother Harold, Edward said: 'I commend this woman with all the kingdom to your protection. Serve and honour her with faithful obedience as your lady and sister, which she is, and do not despoil her as long as she lives of any due honour got from me.' Edward also commended to Harold all his foreign servants: he was either to take them into his own service or to let them return safely home with all their possessions.

This does not amount to a straightforward nomination by Edward of Harold as his heir, for the encomiast, as in duty bound, directs his attention primarily to Edith. But it comes very close. Similarly, in the poem on Edward's death in the chronicle we read: 'Yet the wise ruler entrusted the realm / to a man of high rank, to Harold himself, / a noble earl who all the time / had loyally followed his lord's commands / with words and deeds, and neglected nothing / that met the need of the people's king.'[28] It is the same with the Bayeux Tapestry, which seems to illustrate *Vita*'s text.[29] In the presence of an archbishop, a second man helping the king to sit up in bed and a woman weeping at his feet, Edward stretches out his right arm so as to touch a third man's right hand. On both hands the fingers are fully extended and only the tips are in contact: they do not clasp hands. The legend runs: 'Here Edward in bed addresses his vassals.' And here again we notice the ambiguity. Nevertheless, the 'E' version of the chronicle states baldly, 'And Earl Harold succeeded to the realm of England, just as the king had granted it to him and as he had been chosen to the position' — that is to say, by nomination and election. John of Worcester covers every point: Harold was chosen by

Edward, elected by the whole *witan* and consecrated by Arch-bishop Ealdred. Even William of Poitiers believed that Edward when dying had nominated Harold as his heir.[30] And this may have been so. He could have been under pressure not only from Harold but also from some of the others whom *Vita* claims were ushered into the chamber to hear the king's last words. In the circumstances there was no practical alternative. And a man's last words were awarded considerable authority.

The almost immediate coronation of Harold, which entailed some organization and liturgical preparation, points to an en-visaged conclusion. On the tapestry we read, first, 'Here they gave the crown to Harold', illustrated by two nobles offering the object (but not the one the king had been wearing in bed) to the earl who, however, with his right hand placed firmly on his hip, seems to demur. Nevertheless the coronation follows straight away. The new king is shown enthroned, holding a sceptre in his right hand and an orb in his left, while two nobles and Archbishop Stigand, who is named, display him to an admiring throng. The rubric is: 'Here is seated Harold king of the English.'[31]

The part that a formal election played in the succession to the English kingship at this time is dubious. Many of Harold's predecessors on the throne had gained the position through a *coup d'état* or the support of a faction. But most of the impor-tant men in the kingdom were at court when Edward died, and it would seem that Harold's succession was at least unopposed. Indeed, with its promise of continuity and fair dealing it was most likely popular; and it could rightly be argued that the earl was the choice of the *witan*, the wise men.[32] Even a crowning and consecration by the church was not absolutely essential. It is unlikely that the kings between Æthelred and Edward had all been consecrated; and even Edward had delayed the ceremony for almost a year. There is no doubt, however, that Harold was accorded a sacramental coronation, and on an important church festival, although it is not certain who was his consecrator and what order of service was used.[33] If Stigand was indeed the officiator, it might be expected that the ancient liturgy, the Second English Ordo of 973, would have been used. If, however, Ealdred of York was in charge, it might well have been the Third English Ordo, which Ealdred himself may have composed at Cologne in 1054 while waiting to see Edward 'the Exile', the possible successor to Edward on the throne. And if Stigand was the sole consecrator, the validity of the service could have been impugned, for the archbishop of Canterbury was, if not excommunicate, certainly not in communion with Pope Alexander II, for he had by mischance received his pallium in 1058 from Benedict X, who later was generally regarded as an anti-pope, and had never regularized his position.[34] That Stigand officiated is the view of the Norman sources.[35] John of Worcester, however, believed that Ealdred of York was responsible. The same cleavage of opinion existed over William the Conqueror's coronation a year later.[36] The safest view is that in both cases both archbishops, if available, would have taken part. They would have wanted to; and for the man to be crowned it was *ad majorem cautelam*, the safest course of action.

The verdict of *The Anglo-Saxon Chronicle* was: 'And Earl Harold was now consecrated king and he met with little quiet in it as long as he ruled the realm.' John of Worcester adds a eulogy on Harold's just rule.[37] He seems indeed to have met with no opposition in England; there was no immediate proscription of possible enemies among the nobility and clergy as occurred with the accession of Cnut and his successors, including Edward. And Wales and Scotland made no overt hostile moves. According to Bishop Wulfstan of Worcester's chaplain and biographer, Coleman, as interpreted in Latin by William of Malmesbury, Harold took his episcopal friend on a tour of northern England to help him secure its adherence;[38] and such was the rough northerners' respect for the bishop's sanctity that they suppressed their dislike of the softness of the southerners and mistrust of Tostig's brother, and readily submitted. It is possible that Harold put Siward's son, Waltheof, over part of the earldom in the east midlands.[39] And it may have been at this time that Harold married Ealdgyth, the daughter of the late earl Ælfgar of Mercia, the sister of Earls Edwin and Morcar and the widow of King Gruffydd ap Llywelyn of Wales, although it could have been at any time after 5 August 1063 when Gruffydd was killed.[40] It is not known whether she was crowned queen. The main purpose of the marriage was to strengthen his alliance with the Mercian family and to provide an heir born in the purple and of unquestionable legitimacy.[41] Two children, Harold and Wulf or Ulf, have been ascribed to this union; and if the marriage was in 1066 they would have to have been posthumous twins. Harold presents no problem: he is found again later in credible circumstances. Wulf is not so surely ascribed. The Mercian family had no Scandinavian connections, and a son of Harold with that name suits Edith Swan-neck's brood better. The boy is first noticed as a hostage in William the Conqueror's hands on the king's death in Normandy in September 1087. E.A. Freeman concluded that he must have been taken in February 1070, when William captured Chester, the city to which Ealdgyth had fled in 1066. This is possible; but it should be noticed that the boy would then be probably no more than three years old, and there is no evidence that Ealdgyth and her family were still there at the time. In short, it is not certain who was Wulf's mother.

There was little time for Harold to put his own stamp on the royal government. But it seems that he took over the royal powers without trouble and was an active governor. He was just about forty years old. John of Worcester wrote him an idealized testimonial: 'As soon as he took over the government of the kingdom he began to abolish bad laws and establish good ones, to become the patron of churches and monasteries, to both cherish and venerate bishops, abbots, monks and clerks, to show himself kind, humble and affable to all good men, but hateful to all malefactors, for he ordered earls, satraps (ealdormen) and sheriffs and all his servants to arrest all thieves, robbers and disturbers of the kingdom. And for the defence of the fatherland he himself laboured on land and sea.'[42] There could be no higher praise. William of Malmesbury pronounced more soberly, 'because of his character, if he had obtained the kingdom lawfully, he would have ruled it wisely and bravely'.[43] William of Poitiers gloats over the wealth of Harold's England and the riches in the royal treasury.[44] And in support of these views is that standard measure of a government's effectiveness — its coinage. Harold's is most impressive.[45] His one issue of silver pennies (the only unit in circulation), coined at no less than 44 provincial mints from dies obtained from London, are of excellent quality. His crowned head with a sceptre, a more classical design than usual, faces left (a change from Edward's); and, prominent on the reverse, between two lines across the field, is the word PAX (peace). The significance of this is unknown; but, if it was a manifesto, it was out of luck.

Less well preserved are the products of the royal secretariat which, in these transitional months, must have been working at full stretch. No charter and only one writ, in favour of Bishop Giso of Wells, has survived.[46] They were not of much value in the Norman era. How he treated the earldoms is, therefore, uncertain. Clearly he left Mercia and Northumbria in the hands of the Mercian brothers. As he needed to please his own kin, he may have enlarged the territories under the control of Leofwine and Gyrth at the expense of his own earldom of Wessex, and even endowed therein his nephew Hacon. Certainly the two brothers remained faithful to him to the end. What happened to Hacon is unknown.

Harold returned from York to Westminster at Easter, 16 April.[47] On his travels he had received some moral exhortation from Wulfstan, who believed that the growing prosperity of the country had corrupted its inhabitants, and urged Harold to suppress sin in the kingdom.[48] This echoes Edward's vision on his deathbed of an avenging God. And the theme of a sinful people provides an explanation of the troubles the kingdom was to suffer. Wulfstan was particularly offended by the fashion of long hair among the male aristocracy, and used a little knife he carried for cleaning his nails or scraping stains from books to cut any luxuriant tresses which were bowed before him. He prophesied that those men who wore their hair long like women would be as weak as women in the defence of their land against foreigners.

The forebodings of the dying and the chiding of moralists are unlikely to have had much effect on a man of action like Harold. But shortly after his return from York, on 24 April, Halley's comet appeared in the sky, not to disappear before about 8 June. To most observers it was a portent of disaster. It is shown on the Bayeux Tapestry immediately after the coronation — an artistic foreshortening — 'These men marvel at the star', and is followed by a scene in which someone carrying a sword imports a piece of important news to the king sitting on his throne, while in the lower margin are ghostly unmanned ships floating on the sea. There is no verbal explanation.[49] For Harold and England it was a time of great unease. Yet Harold's behaviour in 1066 is marked by supreme self-confidence. He had achieved, perhaps, even more than he had expected. But, always an opportunist, he may have started to push his luck a little too hard.

Notes

1. *ASC*, 'C', 'D', *s.a.*; John of Worcester, ii. 596–7.
2. *Vita Sancti Gundleii*, cap. 13, in *Lives of the Cambro-British Saints*, ed. W.J. Rees (Welsh MSS Soc., 1853), pp. 153–4; A.W. Wade-Evans, *Vitae Sanctorum Britanniae et Genealogiae* (1944), pp. 184–6.

3. *ASC*, 'C', 'D', *s.a.*; John of Worcester, ii. 596–9; *Vita*, pp. 76–81, 28–9; *FNC*, ii. 487–507.
4. *Vita*, pp. 76–7.
5. Ibid., pp. 28–9.
6. Ibid., pp. 80–3; Renée Nip, 'Political relations between England and Flanders', *ANS*, xxi (1999), 150.
7. *Historia translationis S. Cuthberti*, cap. 5, ed. J. Hodgson Hinde, Surtees Soc., li (1868), 168–70; cf. Symeon, *Historia Ecclesiae Dunelmensis*, ed. T. Arnold (Rolls ser., 1882), pp. 243–5; Barlow, *EC 1000–1066*, pp. 257–8.
8. John of Worcester, ii. 596–9.
9. For the feud, see Walker, pp. 105–7. Stafford, p. 45, believes that this Gospatric was the uncle of the Gospatric who accompanied Tostig to Rome in 1061, and, pp. 270–2, that he was possibly the last surviving son of Uhtred, earl of Bamburh, who had married a daughter of King Æthelred. Ann Williams thinks that Gamal son of Orm was perhaps, confusingly, the son of the Orm Gamal's son, whose wife, Æthelthryth was the daughter of Ealdred, earl of Bamburgh (1019–38) and sister to the second wife of Earl Siward, who died in 1055: 'Thegnly piety and ecclesiastical patronage in the late Old English Kingdom', *ANS*, xxiv, 10–11. For Ulf son of Godwin, see ibid., pp. 11–12.
10. *ASC*, 'D', 'E', *s.a.*
11. *Vita*, pp. 58–61.
12. After the blinding and retirement of Oedipus, king of Thebes, his eldest son, Eteocles (Harold), and his younger son, Polynices (Tostig), agreed to reign in alternate years, Eteocles taking the first. However, when, at the expiry of the term, he refused to make way for Polynices, who had married a foreign wife, the cadet returned with the Famous Seven, and the brothers met and killed each other.
13. *Vita*, pp. 84–7.
14. Ibid., pp. 26–9.
15. R. Beare, 'Earl Godwin's son as a barnacle goose', *Notes and Queries*, ccxlii, 459–62; 'Swallows and barnacle geese', ibid., ccxliii (1998), 5; 'Which of Godwin's sons was called a barnacle goose?', ibid., ccxliv (1999), 5–6; 'Godwin's sons as birds', *Prudentia*, xxxii, 1 (May 2000), 25–52.
16. *Vita*, pp. 78–9.

17. Ibid., pp. 28–9.

18. Ibid., pp. 26–9, 58–9.

19. *Harold*, Act IV, sc. 2, *ad fin.*

20. OV, ii. 170–1.

21. *Vita*, pp. 80–1.

22. *DB*, i. 252ᵛ.

23. *The Anglo-Norman Satirical Poets and Epigrammatists of the Twelfth Century*, ed. T. Wright (Rolls ser., 1872), ii. 149.

24. *Vita*, pp. 50–3.

25. *Carmen*, vv. 642–53.

26. Below, p. 128 and above, p. 85.

27. *Vita*, pp. 116–27; cf. *BT*, pl. xxxii; *FNC*, iii, app., note C, 'Edward's bequest of the crown to Harold', pp. 578–600, especially pp. 585–6.

28. *ASC*, 'C', 'D', *s.a.*

29. Pl. xxxii. *FNC*, as above, n. 27, especially pp. 586–7.

30. John of Worcester, ii. 600–1; *GG*, ii, 11, ed. Chibnall, pp. 118–19, and n. 3; William of Malmesbury, *GR* i, 280, casts doubt on this 'English' view.

31. *BT*, pl. xxxii–xxxiii.

32. *FNC*, iii, app. note D, pp. 600–16.

33. But see Janet L. Nelson, 'The rites of the conqueror', *ANS*, iv (1982), 123–9, 215, n. 52; R. Foreville, 'Le sacre des rois anglo-normands et angevins et le serment du sacre, XIᶜ–XIIᶜ siècles', *ANS*, i (1979), 49–62, at 57–60; cf. also *FNC*, iii, app., notes E and F. For Edward's coronation service, see Barlow, *Edward*, pp. 60–4.

34. Barlow, *EC 1000–1066*, pp. 302–10.

35. *GG*, ii, 1, ed. Chibnall, pp. 100–1.

36. Barlow, *Carmen*, pp. xxxvii–xxxviii, 46–9.

37. John of Worcester, ii. 600–1; and see below, pp. 128–9.

38. *Vita Wulfstani*, pp. 22–3. For the benevolence of Godwin and Harold towards the see of Worcester, see A. Williams, 'The spoliation of Worcester', *ANS*, xix (1997), 400.

39. Walker, p. 141.

40. The marriage was known to William of Jumièges, *GND*, ii. 161–3; John of Worcester, ii. 604–5; Orderic Vitalis, ii. 138–9, 216–17, and Benoît de Sainte-Maure, vv. 36578–36771 — but nowhere dated. Cf. *FNC*, iii, Note K., pp. 638–40.

41. For Harold's children, see *FNC*, iv. 143, 315, 708, 753–4.

42. John of Worcester, ii. 600–1.
43. *GR*, i. 280.
44. *GG*, ii. 30–1, ed. Chibnall, pp. 152–3.
45. G.C. Brooke, *English Coins* (1932), pp. 65–78, pl. xvii, no. 15; also *Vita*, frontispiece.
46. Sawyer, no. 1163.
47. *ASC, s.a.*
48. *Vita Wulfstani*, p. 23.
49. *BT*, pl. xxxiv.

chapter 7

THE COLLAPSE OF
THE DYNASTY, 1066

H arold was fully aware of the dangers he faced from his
enemies after his coronation. Tostig, with the precedent
of the events of 1051–2 in mind, was likely to invade from
Flanders in order to extort the restoration of his earldom. The
duke of Normandy was bound to intervene. A probe might even
be expected from a Scandinavian ruler or adventurer. Harold
quickly gave notice that he would resist his enemies with all the
resources available to him and with all the determination and
valour for which he was renowned. He was supported from the
beginning by at least one brother — possibly Gyrth, although
this one had usually paired with Tostig — and both Gyrth
and Leofwine were with him at the end. Moreover, he could
expect loyalty and support from the whole country, for no class
or individual had anything to gain from his displacement.

Tostig was the first to move. According to Orderic, a rather
late source, he travelled from Flanders to Normandy in an
attempt to gain an ally; but William was not yet ready to get
involved. So Tostig sailed from the Cotentin peninsula and,
because of storms, landed up in Norway, where he successfully
enlisted the king, whom Orderic calls Harold Fairhair, but was
in fact that seasoned adventurer Harold Hardrada, in a joint
enterprise.[1] The Chronicle 'C' and 'D', however, have Tostig

THE COLLAPSE OF THE DYNASTY, 1066

land on the Isle of Wight in May, a much more likely story, and there he extorted both money and provisions. He then, according to 'C', ravaged the English coast until he came to Sandwich. Meanwhile Harold had begun to mobilize his army and navy; and Tostig, after enlisting and press-ganging sailors from Sandwich, hastily sailed north. According to Chronicle 'D', Harold and a brother (unnamed) assembled naval and land forces larger than had ever previously been raised in England; and clearly they were thinking beyond Tostig. In the *Chronica* of John of Oxenedes it is stated that Harold appointed Ælfwold, abbot of St Benet of Hulme (on the sea coast in Norfolk), guardian of the shore.[2] And there is a story in Domesday Book of how Æthelric, lord of Kelvedon (in Essex, between Chelmsford and Colchester) took part in the naval battle against 'King' William, fell sick on his return to London (? in September), and left his estate at Kelvedon to Westminster Abbey.[3]

When the fleet was finally mobilized at Sandwich, Harold took it to the Isle of Wight, where it remained all summer and autumn waiting for an invasion from Normandy which was greatly delayed.[4] He also mobilized his ground forces and stationed them along the English coast which faced the duchy. William of Poitiers maintains that in addition he sent spies to Normandy, one of whom was captured and treated with disdain by the duke.[5] It may be assumed that Harold was aware of the shipbuilding and impressment of vessels and the assembly of weapons and stores, so excellently shown on the Bayeux Tapestry.[6] And, as William was assembling his forces around the mouth of the Dives, Harold was correctly stationing his navy — directly opposite. Still, when provisions ran out for the English forces on 8 September, the campaign season would have seemed to be almost over. The king 'rode inland' and the ships were brought up to London after suffering heavy losses, presumably from a storm on the way.[7]

In fact the warfare was just about to begin. Tostig, with sixty ships, had ravaged Lindsey (the old kingdom south of the Humber, then part of Mercia), only to be driven out by Earls Edwin and Morcar and suffer the desertion of most of his sailors. Left with only twelve small vessels, Tostig sailed on to Scotland, where he was welcomed by King Malcolm and remained all the summer, waiting for one of his brother's more powerful enemies to move. Eventually, either there or at the mouth of the Tyne, he joined forces with Harold Hardrada, who had arrived, it was thought, with no less than 300 ships. Whereas Tostig, a few years younger than his brother Harold, was not yet forty, the king of Norway was elderly for a warrior, just over fifty. According to his own poem, recited in his Saga (cap. 53),

> *Now I have caused the deaths*
> *Of thirteen of my enemies.*
> *I kill without compunction*
> *And remember all my killings.*
> *Treason must be scotched*
> *By fair means or foul*
> *Before it overwhelms me.*
> *Oak trees grow from acorns.*[8]

He also had little respect for the English, claiming 'that people say they are not entirely to be trusted' (cap. 79).

According to Chronicle 'D' and 'E' Tostig became the Norwegian king's vassal; and their joint forces sailed up the Humber and Ouse towards York. At Riccall they disembarked, and, according to the thirteenth-century Icelandic historian, Snorri Sturluson, in his *Heimskringla*, they so smashed a defending army that 'the English dead were piled up so thickly that the Norwegians could cross the swamp with dry feet'. But this appears to be a mistake. It seems in fact that it was not until the invaders reached Gate Fulford on Wednesday 29 September that they first met serious opposition. Then they were attacked by Earls Edwin and Morcar and, perhaps, Waltheof; and although the earls inflicted heavy casualties, they suffered such severe losses themselves that they took no further part in the warfare of that year. The victors then entered York, exchanged hostages, and were provisioned. Apparently they made a pact that they would together march south and conquer the whole country.

Meanwhile 'our king Harold', as Chronicle 'D' calls him, had been hastening up the Roman road, Ermine Street, from London. Nevertheless, one of his thegns (un-named) found time to give land at Paglesham in Essex to Westminster Abbey before accompanying his lord north.[9] Whether it saved his life is not recorded. The two hundred or so miles could have been covered in four days by hard riders leading remounts and requisitioning horses whenever they could. But units of the army, even when mounted, would not be expected to do more than 25 miles a day. The twelfth-century hagiographer, Osbert of Clare, prior of Westminster, tells the story that, while Harold marched north, King Edward appeared in a dream to Abbot Ælfwine of Ramsey (1043–1079/80) and told him to inform the king that his journey would end in victory over the foe.[10] On Sunday 24 September Harold reached Tadcaster on the River Wharfe, some ten miles south-east of York, and there he marshalled his troops in preparation for an assault on the enemy.[11]

On the next day, as Tostig and Harold Hardrada had moved out to Stamford Bridge, eight miles east-north-east of York, Harold passed through the city and caught the enemy by surprise. The one incident reported — and it could be mythical — is that Harold's attack was delayed by a single Norwegian defending the bridge over the navigable River Derwent, a hero eventually removed by a thrust beneath his chain-mail, his byrnie, from an English soldier either creeping or wading under the bridge. There is also mention of an English archer,[12] a matter of interest because the role of archers in English armies of this period is far from clear. Whatever tactics Harold employed — and the sources give the impression of a headlong assault — there was a savage encounter on the far side of the bridge in which both Tostig and Harold Hardrada were killed and their troops, 'Norwegians and Flemings', decimated.

In the end the survivors fled to their ships, perhaps still at Riccall, and there were further casualties from drowning and burning — for some of the vessels must have been set on fire. A mass burial, probably of Scandinavians, has been found here.[13] Finally Harold gave quarter to the survivors, mainly, it seems, those who had not been involved in the battle. These included Olaf, the Norwegian king's son and, according to William of Malmesbury,[14] his other son, Magnus, together with the bishop and Paul Earl of Orkney. With the two Norwegian princes, who succeeded Harold Hardrada as kings of Norway, went also Tostig's two sons, Skuli and Ketil.[15] Harold took oaths of peace and hostages from those he spared and allowed them to leave in some twenty ships. Tostig, whose corpse was recognized by a wart between his shoulders, was buried at York; but according to Orderic Vitalis, writing about 1125, a great mountain of bones still lay on the battlefield in his time, bearing witness to the terrible slaughter on both sides.[16] But Domesday Book, which records quite a few Englishmen killed at Hastings, seems to mention only one, the un-named uncle of Abbot Æthelwig of Evesham (1058–77), killed in 'Harold's battle against the Norse'.[17]

Harold's victory can be contrasted with Edwin and Morcar's defeat. It marked him out as a most distinguished field commander. But in retrospect the battle seemed almost an irrelevance. As the encomiast wrote in despair:

And who will write that Humber, vast and swoll'n
With raging seas, where namesake kings had fought,
Has dyed the ocean waves for miles around
With viking gore, while heaven mourns the crime?
What madman write of this, at which the mind
Grows faint and ears are shocked? Report feels shame
At such a crime. For whom shall I write now?[18]

It was the death of Tostig, whom the poet fails to name, that so affected him, all the more since he knew that the memory of it would distress his patron, the queen. Guy Bishop of Amiens, who wrote a poem, *Carmen*, on William the Conqueror's campaign in 1066, even believed that Harold, another Cain, had himself cut off his brother's head with his sword and buried head and trunk in the ground.[19] It is not impossible that Harold had killed Tostig with his own hand, but more likely that Guy thought it artistically appropriate. It also appears from a late and untrustworthy source that Gyrth was with Harold at Stamford Bridge;[20] and this is quite possible. The whereabouts of Leofwine, however, are unchronicled. It is possible that he commanded the royal fleet.

William duke of Normandy landed at Pevensey in Sussex on 28 or 29 September, that is to say three or four days after Harold's victory. Harold fought with him outside Hastings on 14 October. The king's timetable between the two battles is difficult to establish exactly. It is roughly 250 miles from Pevensey to York, and it would have taken at least five days for the news of William's landing to have reached him in the north, although if he had left Stamford Bridge say two days after the battle, he could have met the messengers perhaps on the second or third of October, and been able to reach London on the fourth or fifth. He could not, of course, have moved large contingents of soldiers, even if they were all mounted, at that speed. To get an army from London to Hastings, some fifty miles, would take at least two days, so that he must have left the city no later than the twelfth. This would give him about a week in London, which is what Ordericus Vitalis allows him.[21] To fight two major battles, 250 miles apart, within nineteen days is an outstanding achievement. For the eleventh century it is impossible to cite its equal.

Such a tight schedule had its impact on the composition and size of the army that Harold could have marshalled at Hastings. He would have reached London with only fragments of the units which had fought at Stamford Bridge and Riccall, probably little more than his housecarls and closest vassals. William of Malmesbury claims that because he had not shared out the spoils of the northern campaign he had been deserted by many.[22] All sources agree, although possibly merely following *Carmen*, that his intention was to push on immediately to attack the duke and, as he was a master of guile, to catch the invader unawares.[23] Orderic Vitalis gives a probably fictitious account of what happened at London.[24] His mother Gytha and his brother Gyrth begged him to wait awhile and rest after all he had just been through. Gyrth even advised him not to take on William: Harold had sworn oaths to the duke and would be disadvantaged if he broke them. He Gyrth would go against William instead. Harold was so infuriated by this advice that when his mother clung to him to keep him back, he kicked her away. Nevertheless, according to the same source, he did spend six days in London attempting to assemble an army with which to confront the duke. William of Poitiers believed that he drew huge forces from the shires.[25] It was also thought that he had stationed a fleet off the coast to prevent William's escape.[26] Although the advice allegedly given him by his family and friends, to wait and see, makes good sense and, as Orderic knew full well, was justified by events, Harold's bold behaviour cannot be condemned out of hand. The author of *Vita* wrote of him, 'the fault of rashness or levity is not one that anyone could charge agsinst him'.[27] The invaders were ravaging his ancestral earldom. And the Battle of Hastings was a very close-run thing.

It had taken William almost nine months to launch his invasion. The delay shows how difficult he found it to recruit enough support for so hazardous an enterprise. He was supported throughout by his half-brothers, Odo Bishop of Bayeux and Robert count of Mortain. But his own resources were few. He had no ships and, as for an army, it is doubtful if his own vassals owed him military service outside the duchy. When he consulted these he found them by no means enthusiastic supporters of his proposal.[28] But there exists a list of ships and knights promised on oath by some of his vassals, lay and ecclesiastical.[29] The ships total 776 and the knights 280; and clearly the duke had to look as well outside the duchy for troops. Eustace II, count of Boulogne, was the most important of his recruits. Soldiers were attracted from Brittany, Maine and Aquitaine.[30] Archers and crossbowmen were hired, but from where is unknown. A diplomatic offensive was mounted and papal support was achieved. All these preparations took time; and when the invasion forces were assembled around the mouth of the River Dives in August, it must have taken some weeks to marshal these motley contingents into an organized and disciplined force. Moreover, in August the winds were contrary. The size of the expeditionary force can only be conjectured. Some 20,000 men and 500 ships would seem to be the top limit; ten thousand effectives is probably closer to the mark.[31]

The delay had worked to William's advantage, for when he sailed from Saint-Valery in Ponthieu, to which harbour he had transferred his forces, to Pevensey in Sussex and occupied the old Roman fort of Anderida, he faced no opposition; and it was the same when he then moved his army to the more strategically placed Hastings. There he waited, reconnoitring and raiding for provisions. His strategic plan is unknown; but it must have envisaged a battle with Harold's forces and ultimately the king's death or expulsion. If so, he needed to fight, like Harold Hardrada, close to his ships, in case of a reverse.

From London to Hastings, by a road which then finished in the forest of Andredsweald on the downs north of Hastings, was more than a day's march for even élite troops. The size of Harold's army is as problematical as that of William's. Both his brothers, Gyrth and Leofwine, had in fact joined him at London; and the core of the English army must have consisted of the housecarls and thegns of the three. Other troops would have joined the king as a result of his summonses to the shires. The thegns of the abbey of Abingdon fought and died in the battle;[32] and men came in as he rode south through Kent and Sussex, parts of his old earldom.

In Domesday Book are recorded the deaths of men from Hampshire, Berkshire, Huntingdonshire, Suffolk and Norfolk.[33] It is indeed possible that some of the troops stationed in the spring to defend the south coast were still in place. William of Poitiers considered that Harold had huge forces which had been reinforced by a large contingent sent by the Danes. The Danish contribution, unless the archdeacon was thinking of housecarls, seems unlikely, although Ordericus Vitalis claims that Swegen of Denmark invaded William's England in September 1069 partly to avenge the losses his men had suffered in Harold's war.[34] But even if Harold's army outnumbered William's, some English observers considered it smaller than it could have been and inadequate for the task.[35]

If Harold hoped to catch the Normans by surprise at Hastings, as he had the Norwegians at Stamford Bridge, he must have intended to attack on the day after he left London. He seems, indeed, to have reached the southern fringe of Andredsweald on the evening of Friday, 13 October. William learnt from scouts of his approach and prepared to march out of his camp in the hope of finding a more favourable battle-ground. *Carmen* describes the exchange of messages by envoys as the two forces came within range, William stating his lawful claim to the English throne, Harold more laconically quoting the Bible (*Gen.*, xvi. 5), that God would decide between them. But these are most likely the poet's inventions. All that is clear is that early on Saturday, 14 October (20 Oct., Gregorian calendar), Harold's army was emerging from the forest on Caldbec Hill, when William's came into sight on Telham Hill. Whereupon the king began to mass his troops about half a mile to the south on the hill on which Battle Abbey now stands; and again, about half-a-mile away, the duke marshalled his troops for an attack. On the tapestry the Norman knights are shown already in mail armour and fully armed before they left Hastings. As it was before the days of horse-armour this is just possible. But, if so, the soldiers would have been far from fresh by the time the battle began. It would seem more likely that they armed on Telham Hill. Harold was no stranger to these parts. Not only were they in Sussex, the family's homeland, but also he held land at Whatlington and Crowhurst, the one to the north and the other to the south of the battlefield.[36]

All the sources agree that the English formed a dismounted phalanx, with their horses coralled in the rear, and faced the enemy with a 'shield-wall', defended mainly with axes and spears. There can be no doubt that the elevated position, fronted by rough uncultivated land and flanked by marshes, was very strong. It was a sort of citadel, easily defensible but, because of the lack of cavalry, without much attacking power. Moreover, because of an apparent shortage of archers (perhaps, because unmounted, some had fallen behind on the march), it was without the means of keeping the attackers at a distance. The tapestry shows English troops throwing missiles of all kinds; but this was a tactic far inferior to the deployment of units of bowmen. In contrast, the invaders could send archers, even the slow-shooting crossbowmen, to inflict casualties on the phalanx from a safe distance.

According to Chronicle 'D', the armies met at the hoary apple tree, possibly a feature which marked the southern boundary of Harold's Whatlington estate, according to Orderic, at Senlac, the sandy brook.[37] Alfred Lord Tennyson called it, more poetically, 'Sanguelac: the Lake of Blood'.[38] It was open countryside. Harold's standard, according to the tapestry, was in the shape of a wyvern (perhaps the Wessex dragon); but William of Poitiers believed that Harold's 'famous banner', which William after his victory sent to Rome in return for the papal banner under which he had fought, displayed an armed man, embroidered with thread of the purest gold.[39] The battle is supposed to have started at 'the third hour', that is to say about 9 a.m., and lasted until night-fall.

The basic account of the battle is 262 verses within 835 lines of a truncated and now unattributed poem (*Carmen*) on William's campaign from his landing at Saint-Valery at the mouth of the River Somme in Ponthieu in September 1066 to his coronation at Westminster at Christmas.[40] Its probable author, Guy Bishop of Amiens (1058–1074/5), was a member of the ruling family of the county of Ponthieu, who earlier had seemingly been archdeacon of that area. He wrote the poem most likely in 1067 and certainly not much later. Although he had no first-hand knowledge of the battle, he knew men who had. His nephew, Hugh, 'the noble heir of Ponthieu' was, according to the bishop, not only a combatant but one of Harold's killers; Bernard lord of Saint-Valery may have accompanied the duke to England;[41] and Guy, who was often at the French royal court, was fully enmeshed in the aristocratic society of northern France and the Low Countries. He knew all about feudal warfare and knew men who fought in it.[42]

The poem was designed to demonstrate the contribution of the county of Ponthieu and of the neighbouring Eustace count of Boulogne, a relation of the Ponthieu family, to William's victory. Accordingly, it minimizes the purely Norman part:

indeed, William is the only Norman featured in it. Guy writes mainly of the French and Bretons. The poem was, therefore, considered inadequate by William of Poitiers, despite his name a true Norman, when he used it as a source for his *Gesta Guillelmi*, a panegyric of the duke. To the best of his ability he 'corrected' the bias, suppressed anything he thought harmful to William's reputation, and inserted details which did honour to the Norman achievement. Apart from these two fairly lengthy accounts, there are brief reports and additional detail (of varying plausibility) in other works, particularly of the twelfth century. And the Bayeux Tapestry, an embroidery probably designed and stitched at Canterbury in the 1070s, illustrates some of the major episodes. But since it is dependent for much of the story on earlier literary sources and for much of the design on traditional Canterbury imagery, it cannot be completely trusted on all its detail.

Unfortunately for the defeated Harold and the English, *The Anglo-Saxon Chronicle* has little to say about the Norman invasion; and no one wrote from a Godwinist point of view. It is the victors who write history. The result is that we have very few facts, and these are presented by supporters of the invasion. Moreover, as *Carmen* was not discovered until 1826 and not fully in print before 1839–40, the views of William of Poitiers had gained such an authority from its long start that the newcomer was largely disregarded as a fanciful derivative. The paucity of information and occasional conflict of evidence has not however prevented generations of historians from reconstructing the progress of the battle, sometimes from hour to hour, if not from minute to minute.[43]

Guy's account of the battle is, unfortunately, not entirely clear, and the opening phase is especially muddled.[44] After the rivals had exchanged threats and pleas by envoys, William marshalled his troops, who were then close to the enemy and already armed, by putting the infantry, archers and some crossbowmen, in the vanguard. These were to assail the English phalanx from a safe distance and then withdraw in favour of the cavalry. But, because of the quickness of events, William was unable to get the cavalry into line (they had presumably been marching in column). Guy follows this admission with a rhetorical paragraph on the horrors of war and another on the position and tactics of Harold's forces: a dismounted phalanx on a hill. Once the English are in position, their trumpets sound the call to battle. Guy then returns to the duke's infantry advancing fearlessly up the hill, led by the commander himself. This results in a hand-to-hand and indecisive encounter.

'With the result hanging in the balance', Guy introduces an episode which his main followers will not accept — the antics of the mounted juggler Taillefer who, riding between the armies, plays with his sword, throwing it high into the air, until he is attacked by an Englishman. Taillefer kills his assailant, decapitates him, and displays his head to his fellow soldiers, who 'exult that the first blow was theirs', and hasten to engage in the fight. After this interlude, Guy's account returns to the attack mounted by the duke. He envisages the army as advancing in three divisions in line, with the French attacking the left, the Bretons the right, and the duke with his Normans in the centre. If the French were attacking the English left, they were on William's right flank, and the Bretons on his left; and this is how William of Poitiers saw it. Each division, it seems, was composed of cavalry fronted by infantry. This first, and possibly a second, assault by the ducal army on the English phalanx inflicted casualties, but was repulsed.

William of Poitiers simplifies the verse account drastically.[45] The duke's attack was organized as a front rank of archers, interspersed with crossbowmen; a second rank of heavier armed infantry in hauberks; and squadrons of mounted knights in support. William was in the centre. This attack led to hand-to-hand fighting, in which the horsemen used swords. And the

English, owing to their numbers and the strength of their position, had the advantage in this first phase of the battle.

So far William of Poitiers largely accepts, but clarifies, Guy's account. The Bayeux Tapestry follows the written sources in its depiction of the order of battle, except that it omits the crossbowmen.[46] It provides a striking picture of the English soldiers forming the shield-wall: tall, slender men, helmeted and in chain-mail to the knees, carrying decorated shields which catch the arrows, and wielding spears and axes. One unprotected English archer bends his bow, and missiles aimed at the duke's cavalry fly through the air. The ground is littered with English corpses. And the next scene, in which four or six stoutly resisting Englishmen are attacked from both sides by horsemen, is labelled, 'Here fell Leofwine and Gyrth, the brothers of King Harold'.[47] In *Carmen* Gyrth appears in a later incident; and neither Guy nor William of Poitiers mentions Leofwine.

There is also a serious disagreement over the next phase of the battle. According to Guy, the invaders, baffled by English resistance, resort to stratagem.[48] The French cunningly pretend to flee as though they were defeated, and the English break ranks and go in pursuit. Whereupon both wings of the ducal army try to break into the now disorganized and gaping English phalanx, while those in feigned flight turn upon their pursuers, but are unsuccessful: then 'the Normans turn tail; their shields protect their backs'. The duke, however, removing his helmet and showing his face to prove that he is still alive, manages to prevent the French and Normans riding off the battlefield and brings them back into the action.

Because *Carmen* implicates Normans in the retreat, William of Poitiers tells a different story.[49] The English resist the first attack so strenuously that the Breton knights and infantry and the other auxiliaries on the left flank turn tail and almost the whole of the duke's battle line gives way, for the Normans think that William has been killed. But the duke, baring his head, rallies the fugitives and brings them back into the fight. Some thousands of the pursuers are then destroyed. And the ducal army is so reanimated that a second general attack is made on the English phalanx. Involved in this are men from Maine, Frenchmen, Bretons and above all, the valourous Normans. But, as the English still resist, the Normans and their allies mount two feigned retreats, each of which entices pursuers who are then rounded up and slain.

The tapestry does not explicitly illustrate retreats, whether real or feigned.[50] Under the legend, 'Here fall English and French together in battle', are shown tumbling horses and unarmed Englishmen on a hill being killed. This scene is followed by 'Bishop Odo, wielding a mace, encourages the young knights', while Eustace of Boulogne points to the duke, who tilts his helmet to show his face. This is an incident on which all the main sources agree.

Modern commentators tend to stress the role of William's archers in turning the battle in his favour, and point to the frieze of bowmen in the lower margin of the tapestry in the last phase of the combat. But the part played by infantry was normally played down by aristocratic observers. The élite of the battlefield were the knights. Guy of Amiens, who provides the most detailed account of the end of the battle, naturally confines his attention to the leading players.[51]

Once William has rallied his troops, for shame they fight better than before; and the duke sets the pace. With his sword he kills many of the enemy. Gyrth, however, is not frightened 'by the lion's face'. He hurls a spear at William's horse so that the rider is forced to dismount. But the duke not only kills Gyrth but continues on foot to massacre the foe. When eventually remounted at the expense of an unwilling knight from Le Mans, he goes on fighting, but is again dismounted, this time by 'the son of Hellox', a man who has never been identified. William also slays this miscreant and is then rescued by

Eustace of Boulogne, who willingly gives him his horse and takes a mount from one of his own household knights. William and Eustace then continue the fight in company. The duke sees Harold on top of the hill fiercely cutting down those attacking him. So William and Eustace, joined by Hugh, 'the noble heir of Ponthieu', and Gilfard (probably the French baron, Robert fitzGilfard), go in support of the king's assailants. William pierces Harold's shield and chest with his lance; Eustace with his sword cuts off his head below the protection of his helmet; Hugh liquefies his entrails with his spear; and Gilfard cuts off his thigh and carries it some distance away.

William of Poitiers will have nothing of this.[52] He may have both disliked the alleged companions of the Conqueror in this act and also thought the act itself unworthy of his hero. He claims that William had three horses (not *Carmen*'s two) killed under him, and three times on foot he avenged the death of his steed. William, he declares, would have dared to fight Harold in single combat. Although Harold was the sort of man poets liken to Hector or Turnus, William, like Achilles, would have taken on Hector, or, like Aeneas, would have taken on Turnus. In this way William of Poitiers rescues his hero from contamination by lesser mortals and associates him with the heroes of antiquity. But he does not tell us how Harold died.

The tapestry, although discreetly, seems to follow *Carmen* here.[53] After the mêlée are shown knights attacking Harold's headquarters. They pass an ugly scene: a dismounted knight is clutching an Englishman in civilian dress by his long hair, and is about to behead him with, apparently, a sword taken from his victim. This may be a reference to *Carmen*'s anecdote of 'the son of Hellox', who killed the duke's horse only to be slain by the duke in revenge.[54] Six ducal knights attack five English soldiers standing on a hill, all of whom have arrows sticking in their shields. One dead Englishman is shown and in the lower margin there is a frieze of archers. Then, under the legend, 'Here king Harold is killed', four knights, one on the left, one in the centre, and two on the right, are shown attacking eleven mailed English soldiers, seemingly standing on the same hill. Four of these stand under a plastic dragon (wyvern) standard.[55] The flanking knights attack with spears, the one in the centre with a sword. Which of their victims is the king is unclear, and is disputed. Four mortally-wounded Englishmen are shown, falling to the ground and there are bodies in the lower margin. In the centre are two imposing warriors. Under the legend, '*Haroldus rex*', stands a mailed soldier holding a shield and a spear in his left hand, while with his right he clutches an arrow which could be thought to be sticking in his head. He recoils slightly. Then, under the words '*interfectus est*' (is slain), appears a warrior dropping his battle axe when slashed on his left thigh by the sword of a mounted assailant.

As this scene is in a heavily restored section of the tapestry its interpretation cannot be based on minutiae. The safest suggestion is that Harold is shown twice in succession, first wounded by an arrow in the head, then cut down by a sword. Finally, after the king's death, his men flee for their lives. And at this point the now mutilated tapestry ends.

The 'arrow in the eye' has been much discussed. The tapestry in its present form shows the arrow passing on the outside of the conical helmet and thereby inflicting no injury to either the eye or the head. This is a restoration following the stitch holes which survived in the dilapidated fabric. It can be compared with a nearby scene at the very end of the tapestry in which a fleeing Englishman is clutching an arrow which is more obviously protruding from his eye. Charles Gibbs-Smith suggested in 1966 that in the Harold scene the designer had originally intended the man to be hefting a spear, just as his colleague is, but the artist may have decided that he did not want any more horizontal lines crossing his composition, so he substituted an arrow after the embroidery of the raised arm had been completed. 'But in the man's eye, the arrow is not, nor was it ever.'[56] These final words would seem to be incontrovertible. However, it should be noticed that in an earlier scene, in the picture of Norman archers advancing to attack, the bowstrings of the two lower soldiers are shown, impossibly, passing behind the shoulders of the archers.[57] It is possible that both here and with the 'arrow in the eye' the artist's design has not been correctly followed at a later stage.

Other early writers do not help much over Harold's death. William of Jumièges, followed by Orderic, believed that he was killed in the first onslaught.[58] This is unlikely, unless Gyrth and Leofwine had sufficient authority to take over the command. William of Malmesbury says that Harold was killed by an arrow in the brain and adds that a knight cut off the king's thigh as he lay on the ground, for which infamy the Conqueror expelled him from his service.[59] The 'arrow in the eye' was taken up by other writers; and the tapestry may be, if not the originator, the popularizer of this story. Neither William of Poitiers nor post-*Carmen* historians have cared much for Guy of Amiens' version.[60] William of Poitiers remarks that on the following day the bodies of the three brothers were found close to each other and that Harold's was recognized by certain marks, not by his face, for he had been despoiled of all adornment.[61] *Carmen* suggests that bodies were being robbed before the end of the battle, and the tapestry shows in the lower margin the dead being stripped of their coats of mail.[62] To the victors the spoils! Later legends explain how the king's disfigured corpse was identified in the heaps of naked victims. There was room for error; and the end of the Godwins is as obscure as their beginnings.

It is a matter for speculation why the battle should have ended in this way. It is clear that at one point, when the invaders were in full flight and were almost chased off the field, the English were winning; and the early writers were sure that it was William's leadership which rescued his forces and enabled them to resume the attack. It may be that it was Harold's inadequacy as a general which prevented him from exploiting the discomfiture of his enemy. A full counter-attack at this point could have been decisive. But for infantry to pursue cavalry would have been difficult. The question remains, why did Harold fight to the death? If he had escaped from the battle — and it was no disgrace for a defeated commander to escape in order to fight again — he could surely have raised another army and, if he did not dare risk a second battle, starve the invader out. William could not easily have maintained his Sussex beach-head over winter. There are several possibilities. It may be that Harold was expecting reinforcements. Hastings has been considered Waterloo without the Prussians.[63] It could be that at the end of the day Harold was too tired to come to a sensible decision. He had been on campaign for a month, and even to stand a whole day in chain mail after a ride from London must have been exhausting. From what we know of the man it would seem unlikely that, affected by the loss of his brothers and of so many of his troops, he became suicidal or chose to die with them. It might be because an exit had become impossible on account of his being surrounded and unable to reach his horses, which could have been taken by deserters. Or he may have thought that he was, if not winning, at least not losing the encounter and that nightfall would soon put an end to the fighting, when a surprise irruption brought him down. It could even be that an arrow out of the blue put an end to him and the battle.

Chance always plays a large part in warfare and a general cannot be held responsible for all his misadventures. Harold may or may not be blamed for getting killed. But he possibly can be censured for risking all on a battle. William, after a more than three weeks' wait on the Sussex coast, must have been at his wits' end over what to do. He wanted a battle and indeed was probably provoking one by ravaging the area, part of the Godwins' ancestral lands. But it was not necessary for Harold to fall into the trap. The threat of an attack would, and did, force the duke to call his foragers in. What happened, it would seem, is that Harold, flushed with his victory in the north, thought that he could deal as successfully with William. And he very nearly did.

Notes

1. OV, ii. 138–41, 142–5. Cf. *King Harald's Saga*, caps 78–9.
2. *Chronica Johannis de Oxenedes, with the history of the abbey of St Benet Holme to 1275*, ed. H. Ellis (Rolls ser., 1859), p. 293; F.M. Stenton, 'St Benet of Holme and the Norman Conquest', *EHR*, xxxvii (1922) 225–35, at p. 233. A. Williams, 'The estates of Harold Godwineson', *ANS*, iii (1981), 179–80. Edith Swan-neck was a benefactor of the abbey, *Chronica*, p. 292.
3. *DB*, ii. 14b.
4. *FNC*, iii, app. note DD, 'The operations of the English fleet in 1066'.
5. *GG*, ii, 4, ed. Chibnall, pp. 106–7.
6. *BT*, pl. xl–xli.
7. *ASC*, 'C', 'D', 'E', *s.a.*
8. *King Harald's Saga*, cap. 53; Harold Hardrada's campaign is described in his Saga, caps 79–94.
9. *DB*, ii. 15a.
10. Marc Bloch, 'La Vie de S. Edouard le Confesseur par Osbert de Clare', *Analecta Bollandiana*, xli (1923), 114. Barlow, *Edward*, p. 262.
11. *ASC*, 'C', *s.a.*
12. Ibid. According to *King Harald's Saga*, cap. 92, the Norwegian king was killed by an arrow in the throat.
13. Reported by Mike Pitts in *The Sunday Times*, News Review, p. 9, of 2 December 2001.
14. *GR*, ii. 311.
15. *FNC*, iii. 375, n. 4; *King Harald's Saga*, cap. 98, where they are not identified as Tostig's sons, and Ketil is surnamed 'Hook'.

16. OV, ii. 168–9.
17. *DB*, i. 177ᵛ.
18. *Vita*, pp. 88–9.
19. *Carmen*, vv. 129–39.
20. *De Inventione Sanctae Crucis*, ed. W. Stubbs (1861), cap. 20; *FNC*, iii. 361 and n.
21. OV, ii. 170–3.
22. *GR*, i. 422.
23. *Carmen*, vv. 247–8, 279–83; OV, ii. 172–3.
24. OV, ii. 170–3, repeated from his interpolation in *GND*, ii. 166–9.
25. *GG*, ii, 16, ed. Chibnall, pp. 126–7.
26. *Carmen*, vv. 318–20; OV, ii. 172–3.
27. *Vita*, pp. 48–9.
28. *GG*, ii, 1, ed. Chibnall, pp. 100–1.
29. E.M.C. van Houts, 'The ship list of William the Conqueror', *ANS*, x (1988), 159–83.
30. Körner, pp. 220–53, is sceptical of these non-Norman troops. He agrees with *GG*, ii, 26, ed. Chibnall, pp. 142–3, that 'Duke William with the forces of Normandy subjugated all the cities of the English in a single day . . . without much outside help'. But this is the arch-deacon's hyperbole at its greatest stretch. K.S.B. Keats-Rohan has written of 'the non-Norman Conquest', *ANS*, xiii (1991), 157–72.
31. Barlow, *Carmen*, pp. lxv–lxvi.
32. *Chron. Abingdon*, ii. 3.
33. *FNC*, iii, app., note HH, 'Names of Englishmen at Senlac'. It is in fact called the Battle of Hastings in *DB*.
34. *GG*, ii, 16, ed. Chibnall, pp. 126–7; OV, ii. 224–7.
35. *ASC*, 'D', 'E'; John of Worcester, ii. 604; W. of M., *GR*, i. 281–2.
36. P.A. Clarke, *The English Nobility under Edward the Confessor*, p. 170; A. Williams (as above, n. 2), p. 184; Walker, p. 184.
37. OV, ii. 172.
38. *Harold*, Act III, sc. 1, *ad fin.*
39. *GG*, ii. 31, ed. Chibnall, pp. 152–3.
40. For the sources, Barlow, *Carmen*, liii–lx.
41. *Carmen*, p. xxxi, n.
42. For Guy, Barlow, *Carmen*, pp. liii–lx.
43. For some accounts, see ibid., p. liv, n. 174. On 7 January 1966 Major-General H. Essame produced an hour-by-hour account of

the battle in *The Weekend Telegraph*. And on 24 April 1966 Field-Marshal Lord Montgomery commented on Harold's generalship in *The Sunday Times Magazine*. Some useful observations on the tactics are in M. Strickland, 'Military technology and conquest: the anomaly of Anglo-Saxon England', *ANS*, xix (1997), 353–82.

44. *Carmen*, vv. 335–422.
45. *GG*, ii, 17, ed. Chibnall, pp. 128–9.
46. *BT*, pl. liv–lxvi.
47. Ibid., pl. lxvii–lxix.
48. *Carmen*, vv. 423–61.
49. *GG*, ii. 17–21, ed. Chibnall, pp. 128–33.
50. *BT*, pl. lxix–lxxiii.
51. *Carmen*, vv. 460–550; Barlow, pp. lxxxii–lxxxiii.
52. *GG*, ii, 22–3, ed. Chibnall, pp. 132–7.
53. *BT*, pl. lxxiii–lxxvii.
54. But cf. D. Bernstein, 'The blinding of Harold', *ANS*, v (1983), 62–3.
55. For Harold's standard and its location, see *Brevis Relatio*, p. 32.
56. *The Times*, 8 October 1966, p. 9.
57. This was pointed out to me in 1966 by Mr Hubert W. Harding of Newton Abbot.
58. *GND*, ii. 168–9; OV, ii. 176–7.
59. *GR*, i. 456.
60. One of the latest commentators, Walker, takes no note of it, although it appears in his bibliography.
61. *GG*, ii, 25, ed. Chibnall, pp. 140–1.
62. *Carmen*, v. 532; *BT*, pl. lxxvi–lxxix.
63. J.H. Round, *Feudal England* (1895), p. 390.

chapter 8

THE DIASPORA,
1066–1098

On 14 October 1066 Harold, Gyrth and Leofwine, as well, apparently, as their uncle, Ælfwig abbot of Newminster at Winchester, lay dead on the battlefield; Tostig had been killed at Stamford Bridge; and the only surviving male of that generation, Wulfnoth, was a hostage in William the Conqueror's hands. Of the sisters, Ælfgifu was dead; but the widowed queen Edith and the nun Gunhild remained, both childless. Only Harold and Tostig seem to have left offspring. The mother of all these, the Danish noblewoman, Gytha, was, however, still alive and active.

What happened to the bodies of Gyrth and Leofwine is unknown. No church claimed their burial; and if they were unmarried they were probably left with most of the other fallen to be eaten by worms and the scavengers of the battlefield. The early-thirteenth-century author of the fictional *Vita Haroldi*, presumably a Waltham monk, has Gyrth, who was born about 1032, reappear in King Henry II's reign (1154–89). He relates that Abbot Walter (of Ghent, 1184–1201) interviewed Gyrth at a royal court at Woodstock about Harold's burial; and Gyrth, both then and later at Waltham, denied that Harold was buried there.[1]

The fate of Harold's body was from the beginning, no doubt because of ignorance, the stuff of legend. According to *Carmen*,[2] the duke had the mangled corpse reassembled and wrapped in purple linen, and then took it back with him to his base camp at Hastings. The late king's mother, Gytha, sent to the Conqueror to ask for her son's body, and offered to pay its weight in gold. But William refused; he had decided to have it buried on the cliff overlooking the harbour. The burial was entrusted to a relative of Harold's, a man part-English, part-Norman. This man, whom William of Poitiers identifies as William Malet, lord of Graville at the mouth of the Seine,[3] interred Harold on the cliff under a tombstone on which was inscribed: 'You rest here, King Harold, by order of the duke, so that you may still be guardian of the sea and the shore.' Guy attributes the irony to the duke himself. The whole episode, this pagan tumulus burial conducted by Harold's *compater*, William Malet, is puzzling. There is no trace of Malet in England before the Conquest, and how he could have been a co-father of Harold is unascertainable.

The later history of the body is no less uncertain. William of Malmesbury, writing in the 1120s, believed that the Conqueror had, despite the earlier story, surrendered the body gratis to Gytha, who had then had it buried in her son's foundation at Waltham.[4] The church itself made this claim after its reform in 1177:[5] the community had sent two of its canons, Osgod Cnoppe and Æthelric Childemaister, to accompany the king when he called in on his march from York to Hastings; and these after the battle persuaded William to let them have the corpse. But in order to identify it among the heaps of the slain they had to send for Edith Swan-neck. They then took it back to Waltham for burial. Although the fabric of the church has suffered many vicissitudes since the eleventh century, a tenuous belief that Harold was buried there persisted. In the late eighteenth century, when 'the famous Bumper-Squire Jones' inhabited the adjacent manor house, it was claimed that, during excavations to enlarge the cellar, a coffin bearing the inscription 'Haroldus Rex' was discovered. Jones kept it on show in his cellar. But the house was destroyed by fire shortly after his death and the ruins were completely demolished in 1770.[6]

A more recent claimant to have the bones is Bosham church in West Sussex. On 7 April 1954 a large stone coffin containing some fractured bones, but no skull and apparently only one femur, was excavated under the chancel arch; and in 1996 a local resident claimed that these were the remains of King Harold.[7] But it is difficult to imagine how or why they could have travelled those sixty or so miles to the other end of the shire. In 1066, according to Domesday Book, the manor was held by Earl Godwin, who died in 1053. Although which of his family in fact possessed it remains uncertain, even if it was his widow Gytha, it cannot have been a location attractive to the Conqueror. The one thing that can be said in its favour is that the holder of the church and its considerable estates in 1066 was Osbern, the brother of William fitzOsbern, William's distant kinsman, his steward and friend, whom he made earl of Hereford in 1067. Osbern had lived for long in England, had served in Edward the Confessor's household (to whom also he was related) and had received the church as part of his reward. In 1071 William made him bishop of Exeter, and Osbern took the chapelry with him. William could have regarded him as a safe guardian of Harold's body; and it was probably Osbern who inserted in his church the 'noble' chancel arch illustrated on the Bayeux Tapestry, under which the sarcophagus was unearthed.[8] Nevertheless, Bosham's claim to the body seems weak.

One church which never claimed possession is Battle Abbey. This Benedictine church, dedicated to St Martin, was built shortly after the battle on the field itself, with its high altar supposedly on the very spot where Harold had raised his standard and been killed, although the hill was much reduced in height in order to accommodate the buildings. According to *Carmen*, the Conqueror sorrowed over Harold's bones when buried at Hastings and distributed alms to 'Christ's poor'. He then founded the abbey as a more substantial penitential act for all the victims of the battle. But it is nowhere suggested that a search for Harold's body was made for its enhancement.

It can be thought that as William was a religious and God-fearing man he would not have refused Christian burial to his rival.[9] William of Poitiers expressly corrects the poem's statement that, although the duke had his own casualties buried, he left the English to be eaten by worms and wolves, by birds and dogs. The archdeacon claimed that although William could have done this, he gave free licence to those who wished to bury their dead.[10] Accordingly, William would have surrendered Harold's body to either Gytha or the Waltham canons. In either case, on the assumption that the right corpse was identified on the battlefield, the king would ultimately have been laid to rest in the canonry he had founded presumably for that very purpose. William's relatively generous, if careful, treatment of another rival, Edgar Atheling, who surrendered to him at the end of 1066, can be adduced in support. On the other hand, William was a hard and ruthless man. It is clear that he regarded Harold as a perjurer who had defrauded him of his rightful inheritance. William had fought under a papal banner against an evil man. His position in England until at least 1070 was insecure, and he would not have wanted to surrender an object which could serve as a rallying point for English dissidents. The matter cannot be determined.

Perhaps because there was so much uncertainty over how and when Harold died and what happened to his corpse, legends about his survival soon appeared. By the beginning of the thirteenth century there were even doubts at Waltham itself over its possession of Harold's ashes. The author of *Vita Haroldi* told the story of Harold's survival of the Battle of Hastings which he claimed to have had from a hermit named Saebeorht, who had been for many years a servant of Harold.[11] The king, severely wounded, but not killed, was rescued from the battlefield by a woman and taken to Winchester, where he was tended for two years in a cellar by an Arab woman. He then travelled widely in Europe before returning to England and finishing life as a hermit at Chester. The author expressly rejects the accounts of Harold's death offered by William of Malmesbury and Ailred of Rievaulx, and denies that the king was buried at Waltham. He even, as we have seen, has Harold's 'aged' brother Gyrth, another survivor, deny Waltham's claim.

The true survivors of Harold's generation were his sisters Edith and Gunhild and his youngest brother, Wulfnoth. The Conqueror, according to *Carmen*, after his victory at Hastings, while negotiating the surrender of cities and towns in the south of England from *Fracta Turris* (perhaps Faversham in Kent), sent to Winchester, which Edith held in dower, to demand the payment of tribute. And the queen and the city fathers complied.[12] Thus began an alliance which was to last for the rest of her life. It would seem that William left Edith in full possession of all her lands; and the queen appears to have kept clear of all the conspiracies and rebellions which were to trouble the first decade of his rule. William of Poitiers, probably exaggerating, puts her support for the Conqueror in more positive terms.[13] He makes her an ally of Tostig in 1065–6. Totally unlike Harold, who was stained with lust and murder, avid for riches and plunder, and an enemy of justice and goodness, she could only fight against him with prayers and counsel. She was also a supporter of William. Endowed with masculine wisdom, and knowing, and honouring in her life, what was good, she wanted the man her husband had chosen and adopted as his son to succeed him on the throne, William the wise, the just and the strong. Edward's concern on his deathbed for Edith's future, as reported in *Vita*, lends a little support. He feared that she might be robbed after his death and expressly ordered Harold to treat her well and protect her from despoilers.[14]

Be all that as it may, after the Conquest Edith had large estates in Wiltshire and seems to have lived quietly at Winchester or thereabouts, at times in her old home, the nunnery at Wilton which she had rebuilt. She was in the city in March 1071 when Walcher, a Lotharingian clerk, was brought to be consecrated bishop of Durham. Noting his milky white hair, his rosy face and his great height, she exclaimed, 'Here we have a beautiful martyr' — a prophecy, William of Malmesbury thought, typical of an extravagant nation much addicted to soothsaying.[15] But Walcher was, indeed, murdered on 14 May 1080. Also about 1070–2 she demonstrated her independence and bold spirit by visiting her old friend, Archbishop Stigand of Canterbury, in prison after his deposition by the ungrateful Conqueror.[16] Edith is noticed again on 23 February 1072 when she and her household, seated on the 'up-floor' at Wilton, presumably a gallery in the church, witnessed a sale of land to Giso, Bishop of Wells.[17] She had preserved an apparently total English entourage. She died at Winchester, probably in her mid fifties, a week before Christmas 1075; and the king had her buried with honour near her late husband in Westminster Abbey,[18] although the nunnery at Wilton might be thought more suitable.

Godfrey of Cambrai, prior of Winchester Cathedral (1082–1107), wrote of her in his *Epigrammatica historica*, number 4:

> *The nobility of your forbears magnified you, O Edith,*
> *And you, a king's bride, magnify your forbears.*
> *Much beauty and much wisdom were yours*
> *And also probity together with sobriety.*
> *You teach the stars, measuring, arithmetic, the art of the lyre,*
> *The ways of learning and grammar.*

An understanding of rhetoric allowed you to pour out speeches,
And moral rectitude informs your tongue.
The sun burned for two days in Capricorn
When you discarded the weight of your flesh and went away.[19]

Thus she was remembered at Winchester as an exponent of the seven liberal arts, the stock medieval scholastic curriculum, consisting of the more advanced *quadrivium*, astronomy, geometry, arithmetic and music, and the elementary *trivium*, dialectics, grammar (the Latin language) and rhetoric. To Godfrey she seemed a moral blue-stocking, perhaps moralistic and a little too free with her opinions.

The only other member of the family who continued to live in England was Harold's daughter, Gunhild. She had become a nun at Wilton and was cured of a tumour which had damaged her eyes by Bishop Wulfstan of Worcester (1062–95), who made the sign of the Cross over her when visiting the abbey.[20] She was still at Wilton under Abbess Christina, a daughter of Edward 'the Exile', King Æthelred's grandson.[21] Another woman there was Christina's niece, Edith, the daughter of King Malcolm of Scots and (Saint) Margaret. Malcolm had apparently wanted to marry Edith to the old, but extremely wealthy, Breton lord of Richmond, Alan the Red (Rufus), a son of Eudo Count of Ponthièvre in Brittany. But instead, about 1093, Alan 'abducted' Gunhild from the cloister, having presumably met and preferred her when inspecting Edith. Gunhild, then probably in her thirties, lived with him until his death, which occurred soon afterwards.

A further oddity in the story is that Alan, who was a second cousin of the Conqueror, is thought to have been the commander of the Breton contingent in the duke's army at Hastings and subsequently was in constant attendance on William when king. Moreover, it was his brother Brien who had driven Gunhild's brothers out of Devon.[22] But time is a great healer;

and on Alan the Red's death Gunhild, clearly preferring the pleasures of the secular world to the more limited diversions of the cloister, contemplated marriage with the third son of the Breton count, Alan II, the Black (Niger), the other Alan's younger brother and heir. Meanwhile King Malcolm had seemingly attempted to get King William Rufus to marry his daughter. But Rufus too, after a visit to Wilton, shied off; and Edith was left to marry his brother and successor, Henry I, in 1100, a fate possibly even worse.

We know of Gunhild's remarkable adventures mostly from two long letters written to her by Archbishop Anselm of Canterbury shortly after his consecration at the end of 1093.[23] In the first, Anselm urges Gunhild, who was living in sin with a husband who, the archbishop hopefully suggests, was about to despise and repudiate her, to return to the cloister although she was no longer a virgin. Before the second letter Alan Rufus had died, Gunhild had written to Anselm, and she and the archbishop had had a meeting. She claimed that she had never made a formal profession as a nun before a bishop and therefore was not legally bound to the monastic order, and also that a promise to her of an abbacy had not been honoured. Anselm dismissed the first plea as a technicality; the second he could have regarded as unworthy of his notice. As she was by then involved with Alan the Black, the archbishop prophesied that God would similarly punish him by death if they married. He still wanted her to return to Wilton. Unfortunately we do not know what she decided to do, or how she ended. But as Alan the Black died in 1098,[24] her conjugal experience was short.

In defence of the behaviour of both Gunhild and Edith of Scots it should be noticed that many noblewomen, like the former's aunt, Queen Edith, were put into nunneries simply for their education, or, after 1066, to avoid molestation by the Norman conquerors. And their status could be ambiguous. The girls themselves could have fluctuated in their attitude towards a religious vocation. Hence, unsurprisingly, prayers were not asked for Gunhild, nor apparently for Queen Edith, when the mortuary roll (in modern terms, the book of condolences) of Abbot Vitalis of Savigny reached Wilton about 1110. The convent did, however, proclaim its literary credentials by contributing some verses.[25]

Two members of the family were hostages in Normandy. Wulfnoth, probably Godwin and Gytha's youngest son, born perhaps about 1036, had been given by Edward to Duke William seemingly in 1051, either for safe-keeping or, since the king was childless, as a pledge for their agreement about the succession. He was not released to Harold when his brother came to terms with William in 1064/5, but was taken (with Earl Morcar) by William Rufus when, with his father's blessing, he left his deathbed outside Rouen in September 1087 to dash to England and seize the throne. At Winchester Rufus put Wulfnoth into safe custody; and the earl seems to have remained there or thereabouts under restraint until his death.[26] It is surprising, and some measure of the Godwins' prestige, that Wulfnoth should still be regarded as a prize and a possible danger 21 years after the Norman conquest. Rufus was an honourable man, imbued with the virtues of nascent chivalry, and it is unlikely that Wulfnoth's captivity was other than honourable. He is mentioned a few times during the reign. Near the end of a long list of notables purporting to witness a forged charter of Bishop William of Durham in 1082 appears 'Wulfnoth, brother of King Harold'. And he attests a royal charter dated at Hastings, probably in January 1091, confirming Bishop Osmund of Salisbury's reorganization of his church. William of Malmsbury, however, has him grow old in chains at Salisbury. Orderic Vitalis has him die at Salisbury, but ignores the chains. He was, however, well known to Geoffrey of Cambrai, prior of nearby Winchester Cathedral, for he appears number 12 in the list of 19 notables, ranging from King Cnut to William of Rots, abbot of Fécamp, celebrated with obituary verses in his *Epigrammatica historica* (Historical Epigrams).[27]

The epigram on Wulfnoth (in translation), is:

> *The nobility of his forbears, his simple manners,*
> *His sound views and honourable judgements,*
> *The strength of his body and the fire of his intellect,*
> *All these glorify Earl Wulfnoth.*
> *Exile, prison, darkness, inclosure, chains*
> *Receive the boy and forsake the old man.*
> *Caught up in human bonds he bore them patiently,*
> *Bound even more closely in service to God.*
> *In spring while the Fishes were warmed by the February sun*
> *The ninth day under Hermes was the last for him.*

It would seem that he spent some time in the Winchester cloister and may even have become a monk. The dating clause in the poem does not provide the year of his death. But from the earl's position in the series of poems, a date of about 1094, when Wulfnoth would have been about 58, would seem likely.

Harold's son, Wulf, whose mother is uncertain, was a hostage in William the Conqueror's hands when the king died in the church of St Gervase outside Rouen on 9 September 1087.[28] The king's eldest son, Robert Curthose, who succeeded him in the duchy, then released the prisoners. Wulf and Duncan, the son of Malcolm III of Scots, he knighted before letting them go. Duncan joined Rufus in England, disputed the succession to his father's throne with Donald Bane, and wore the crown for six or seven months in 1094 before being treacherously killed. But Wulf is not noticed again. Perhaps he had thrown in his lot with Duncan.

All the other members of the family seem to have taken refuge abroad, mostly either in Ireland with Diarmait mac Máel na mBó, king of Leinster, or in Scandinavia. In Ireland Diarmait had conquered Dublin in 1052 and assumed the 'kingship of the foreigners', which he soon relinquished to his son, Murchad, the ancestor of the Mac Murroughs.[29] In Denmark there ruled from 1047 until 1074 Swegen Estrithson or Ulfson, a nephew of the great King Cnut and the first cousin of Godwin and Gytha's children. In Norway after Harold Sigurdsson's (Hardrada) defeat at Stamford Bridge in 1066, the two sons who escaped from that disaster, Magnus II (1066–9) and Olaf III (1067–93) ruled in turn. Olaf's son, Magnus III (Barefoot) followed, 1093–1103. Swegen Estrithson was the one remaining member of that large Anglo–Danish extended family capable of challenging William the Conqueror. In the autumn of 1069 he dispatched a fleet of 240 ships to invade England.[30] In command of the expedition were his brother Osbeorn, who had lived in England when his brother Beorn was one of Edward's earls, and the king's sons, Harold and Cnut, who were to reign after him. On 8 September, like Tostig and Harold Hardrada in 1066, Osbeorn entered the Humber and was welcomed by Edgar Atheling and some other remnants of the English resistance. But after York had been sacked the Danes sailed home with the plunder. Conquest, they realized, was beyond their reach.

It was the same again in 1075, when Cnut invaded with more than 200 ships to join in the great revolt against William.[31] He arrived when the rebellion was already collapsing, and once more gained nothing but booty. He had, however, acquired the ambition to conquer, and when king (1080–6) planned a great coalition which included his father-in-law, Robert the Frisian count of Flanders, and Olaf III of Norway. When news of Cnut's preparations reached William in 1085 he took them most seriously and put England on a siege footing. In June, however, Cnut was murdered in the church at Odense and the invasion fleet never sailed. The main result was the Conqueror's Domesday survey. The Norwegians had made even less effort than the Danes to upset the Norman conquest. In 1096

Magnus III, 'Barefoot', as we shall see,[32] reconnoitred the Irish Sea to no avail. But both sets of kings had done the best they could for their dispossessed and exiled English relatives and quasi fellow countrymen.

Earl Godwin's widow, Gytha, after negotiating with William for the body of her son, King Harold, seems to have taken refuge in Devon, probably at Exeter. It is possible that she was still holding most of her dead husband's estates and, if so, was a very wealthy woman. William attacked this city early in 1068; and when it surrendered she and 'many distinguished men's wives', according to Chronicle 'D', retreated to Flat Holme, an island in the Bristol Channel, and stayed there for some time before sailing with a large treasure she had assembled to Saint-Omer. She may have been accompanied on these adventures by her daughter Gunhild; and in her entourage was Blacman, a rich priest who held land of Abingdon Abbey. For Gytha and the priest, Flanders may have been the end of the journey.[33]

Gunhild, Harold's much younger sister, led a very different life from her mother and her elder sister, Queen Edith. According to a memorial inscription in Latin on a small sheet of lead (about 9×7 inches) found in the now destroyed cathedral church of St Donation at Bruges in 1786,[34] Gunhild, born of the most noble parents, Earl Godwin, who ruled over the greater part of England, and Gytha, scion of a most distinguished Danish family, when a girl took a vow of chastity and refused marriage to many noble princes. After the Conquest she lived for some years in exile at Saint-Omer in Flanders, from there moving to Bruges and then to Denmark, before returning to Bruges where she died on 24 August 1087. Always a virgin, she practised the monastic virtues cheerfully and modestly. She was an exemplary Christian. It seems that she gave the church at Bruges, among other holy relics, the mantle of St Bride (Brigit) of Kildare, which may have come from the visits of her brothers or nephews to Ireland, as well as a psalter with Anglo–Saxon glosses. On the evidence of Domesday Book she had been endowed with two substantial manors in Somerset.[35]

Tostig is said to have been accompanied by his wife and their 'suckling' children when he went into exile in Flanders, his wife's homeland, at the end of 1065.[36] As he and Judith were married in 1051, the family's encomiast is obviously exaggerating the helplessness of their offspring; and in the following year, after the battle of Stamford Bridge, as we have seen,[37] Skuli and Ketil were taken by Olaf and Magnus, the sons of the slain Harold Hardrada, back with them to Norway. When king (1067–93), Olaf made grants of land to both brothers, who settled down and became heads of families.[38] Their mother, Judith, who had probably stayed in Flanders after the family's flight there, also moved north, but only as far as Denmark; and in 1072, two years before the death of Swegen Estrithson, she married Welf IV, duke of Bavaria and an ancestor of the House of Brunswick. On her deathbed she bequeathed some relics and treasures, including manuscripts, to the monastery of Weingarten, near Lake Constance in southern Germany. One of the manuscripts, 'The Gospel Book of Countess Judith', was probably made for her and illustrated by an English artist in England before 1065. A representation of Christ's Crucifixion, on fo.16, may well show the countess clinging to the cross.[39]

Harold's children were rather more involved in English history. The king had had two 'wives', Edith Swan-neck and Ealdgyth of Mercia. Whether the first of these was still alive in 1066 and what happened to her is unknown. She had given him at least three sons, Godwin, Edmund and Magnus. Another of his sons, Wulf or Ulf, may also have been hers.[40] And there were at least two daughters, Gytha and Gunhild. Godwin and Edmund, with perhaps Magnus, fled after Hastings to Ireland and took refuge with Diarmait mac Máel na mBó, king of Leinster, with whom their father and uncle Leofwine had sojourned in 1051–2.[41] They could not, however, repeat their seniors' triumphant return.[42] In 1068, with 52 ships, they attacked Bristol and then the Somerset coast. They defeated a local force and killed its commander, Eadnoth the Staller, a former servant of their father, and the father of Queen Edith's steward, Harding; and then, after some further harrying, they returned to Ireland. In June of the following year with a slightly larger fleet they again attacked the western peninsula, first appearing in the Bristol Channel and then ravaging in Devonshire, even attacking Exeter. This time they were met by Brien, one of the sons of Eudo count of Ponthièvre and the Conqueror's lieutenant in the south-west, who destroyed most of their forces and decisively drove them out.[43] It is obvious that they attracted no substantial support and were generally regarded simply as freebooters.

According to northern sources,[44] two sons and a daughter of Harold, presumably Godwin, Edmund and Gytha, took refuge with their kinsman, Swegen Estrithson, king of Denmark. Eadric, 'master of King Edward's ship', also fled there.[45] They could have travelled via Flanders, even escorting their grandmother, Gytha, and aunt Gunhild to that haven. Nothing more is heard of the men; but Gytha was given in marriage by Swegen to Vladimir II, Grand Prince of Kiev, across the Baltic in Russia. Vladimir is said to have been the son of King Jaroslaf and Ingegerd, daughter of King Olaf of Sweden. By Vladimir, Gytha had seven sons and three daughters, and, according to Freeman, from her granddaughters Malfrid and Ingebiorg, daughters of her eldest son Mstislav-Harold, 'most of the kings of the north seem to have sprung'.[46] Harold and Edith Swan-neck's third son, Magnus, may have reappeared in Suffolk. On the outer wall of the rebuilt church of St John sub Castro in Lewes have been placed the remains of a monument, formerly in the churchyard, assigned to Magnus, son of Harold II 'with an inscription mostly in Anglo-Saxon characters' commemorating a hermit, Magnus, 'of the royal Danish line, who had served the church'.[47]

Harold's second wife, Ealdgyth, was collected by her brothers, Edwin earl of Mercia and Morcar earl of Northumbria, in London after the Battle of Hastings and, pregnant, was taken to Chester for her safety.[48] There she gave birth to a son, named after his father, or to twins, if Wulf was indeed her child. From Chester she could have sailed to Ireland and thence to anywhere of her choice. But she is not heard of again, and Harold does not reappear until thirty years later when he was closely attached to the Norwegian royal court. According to William of Malmesbury, he had been welcomed there by Magnus II, Harold Hardrada's son, because the boy's father, Harold Godwinson, had treated him so well in 1066.[49] In 1098, at the age of 33, Harold Haroldson accompanied Magnus II's successor, Magnus III, 'Barefoot', king 1093–1103, with a small fleet, on a visitation of the islands which formed part of his empire, including the Orkneys, the Hebrides and the Isle of Man.[50] For some reason Magnus continued to sail south to the Menai Straits and Anglesey. And there he collided with an Anglo–Norman force led by Hugh earl of Chester and Hugh of Montgomery earl of Shrewsbury[51] which, having defeated the Welsh princes, was ravaging Anglesey. These opposed Magnus when he tried to land, and in the skirmish Hugh of Montgomery was killed by a missile directed from one of the ships. The Norwegians then sailed away. And that is the last that is heard of Harold Haroldson.

In connection with the disappearance from record of the sons of King Harold, E.A. Freeman wrote:[52] 'The family which in two generations had risen from obscurity to the highest pitch of greatness was, in the third generation, so far as history is concerned, utterly wiped out.' Nevertheless, one son of Harold and two of Tostig flourished in Norway and carried the family's genes into a forgetful northern aristocracy; and there could have been further generations also in Ireland. It would seem unlikely that so adventurous a race could simply die out. And, moreover, the achievements of their ancestors were of a kind to be honoured. Godwin may have been clever rather than heroic and there may have been a streak of craftiness in Harold's career. But neither life seems to have been stained by treachery or atrocities. Godwin's treatment of Alfred, Edward the Confessor's younger brother, although perhaps culpable, was probably unduly blackened by his enemies. Harold, especially, gives the impression of being both an honourable man and one who enjoyed life to the full. A lover of wealth and a lover of women, a good soldier when necessary and capable of magnanimity in victory, he probably was, as the librettist of the Bayeux Tapestry viewed him, a hero, although from the Norman point of view doomed by a flaw. And although Anglo–Danish, and with the Danish strain dominant, he has continued to be regarded by the English as a national hero.

Notes

1. *Vita Haroldi*, trans. Swanton, pp. 34–5.
2. *Carmen*, pp. 34–5.
3. *GG*, ii, 25, ed. Chibnall, pp. 140–1. If Malet was part English, his mother must have been English, and she could have held land in the kingdom. Malet is given an important role in most fiction set in this period.
4. *GR*, ii, 306–7.
5. *The Waltham Chronicle*, ed. and trans L. Watkiss and M. Chibnall (1994), pp. 46–56.
6. Dinah Dean, *Evidence of the burial of King Harold II Godwinsson at Waltham Abbey* (undated pamphlet), p. 7.
7. J. Pollock, *Harold: Rex. Is King Harold buried in Bosham Church?* (Penny Royal Publications, 1996).
8. *DB*, i, 16, 17r–v; A.J. Taylor, 'Belrem', *ANS*, xiv (1992), 3–5, n. 4, pl. la and b.
9. For example, M. Chibnall, *The Waltham Chronicle*, p. xlv; Ann Williams, *The English and the Norman Conquest* (1955), pp. 129–30.
10. *GG*, ii, 26, ed. Chibnall, pp. 142–3.

11. Ed. W. de Gray Birch (1885); cf. M. Ashdown (1959) 'An Icelandic account of the survival of Harold Godwinson', *The Anglo-Saxons*, ed. P. Clemoes, pp. 122–36.

12. *Carmen*, pp. 36–9. For *Fracta Turris* and Faversham, *GG*, 28.

13. *GG*, ii, 8, ed. Chibnall, pp. 114–15.

14. *Vita*, pp. 122–5.

15. *GR*, ii, 331.

16. William of Malmesbury, *De Gestis Pontificum Anglorum* (Rolls ser., 1870), p. 37.

17. F.H. Dickinson, 'The sale of Combe', *Proc. of the Somerset Arch. and Nat. Hist. Soc.*, xxii (1876), 106–13; Stafford, p. 109; Barlow, *Vita*, p. 139.

18. *ASC*, 'D', 'E', *s.a.*

19. *The Anglo-Latin Satirical Poets and Epigrammatists of the Twelfth Century*, ed. T. Wright (Rolls ser., 1872), ii, 149. For the scholastic curriculum, see Barlow, *EC 1066–1154*, ch. VI.

20. *Vita Wulfstani*, pp. 34, 84.

21. Barlow, *William Rufus*, pp. 309–16.

22. Below, p. 169.

23. *S. Anselmi Opera Omnia*, ed. F.S. Schmitt (1946–52). Letters, nos 168–9.

24. *Early Yorkshire Charters*, ed. C.T. Clay, iv, *The House of Richmond* (1935), 7.

25. *Rouleau Mortuaire du B. Vital, abbé de Savigni*, ed. L. Delisle (Paris, 1909), pl. xxxviii, tit. 153.

26. Barlow, *William Rufus*, pp. 65–6; H.S. Offler, *Durham Episcopal Charters, 1071–1152* (Surtees Soc., clxxix, 1968), 20; *Regesta Regum Anglorum 1066–1154*, i, ed. H.W.C. Davis and R.J. Whitwell (1913), no. 319; *GR*, i. 245; OV, ii. 178–9.

27. *The Anglo-Norman Satirical Poets and Epigrammatists of the Twelfth Century*, ed. T. Wright (Rolls ser., 1872), ii. 148.

28. Barlow, *William Rufus*, p. 50n.

29. Séan Duffy, 'Ireland's Hastings: the Anglo–Norman Conquest of Dublin', *ANS*, xx (1998), 76–7.

30. D.C. Douglas (1964) *William the Conqueror*, New Haven and London: Yale University Press, pp. 218–22.

31. Ibid., pp. 231–3.

32. Below, p. 170.

33. *FNC*, iv. 140–8; A. Williams, 'The estates of Harold Godwineson', *ANS*, iii (1981), 177; *Chron. Abingdon*, i. 484, 490; *FNC*, iv. 143–4 and n.

34. Latin text in *FNC*, iv, app. M, pp. 754–5. The object is now in St Salvator's Cathedral, Bruges, in the first room of the museum.

35. N. Rogers, 'The Waltham Abbey Relic List', *England in the eleventh century*, ed. C. Hicks (1992), 166–7; Walker, pp. 35, 193. For her lands, *Exon DB*, 96, 99; *DB*, i, 86ᵛ, 97.

36. *Vita*, pp. 82–3.

37. Above, p. 138.

38. *FNC*, iii. 375–6, n. *King Harald's Saga*, cap. 98.

39. See R.W. Southern, *The Making of the Middle Ages* (1953), frontispiece and pp. vii, 78. The MS is now in New York, Pierpont Morgan Library, no. 709.

40. *FNC*, iv, app. M, 'The children of Harold'. Freeman believed that Wulf was Ealdgyth of Mercia's twin son.

41. Above, p. 59.

42. *ASC* 'D', *s.a.* 1067. *FNC*, iv, app. Y, 'The expeditions of Harold's sons'. B. Hudson, 'The family of Harold Godwineson: a study in late Saxon politics', *Royal Soc. of Antiquaries of Ireland*, cix (1979), 92–100.

43. For Brien, see K.S.B. Keats-Rohan, 'William I and the Breton contingent in the non-Norman Conquest, 1060–1087', *ANS*, xiii (1991), 157–72, at pp. 159–61.

44. Walker, pp. 193–5.

45. *DB*, ii. 200.

46. *FNC*, iv. 159, 752–3; and cf. the genealogical table, 'King Harold and his descendants', in Walker, p. xiv.

47. *Lewis's Topographical Dictionary of England*, vol. L–R, p. 77b and information kindly given me by Miss Dinah Dean of Waltham Abbey.

48. John of Worcester, ii. 604–5.

49. *GR*, ii. 318.

50. Barlow, *William Rufus*, pp. 389–90.

51. *GR*, ii. 318, 376.

52. *FNC*, iv. 244.

EPILOGUE

The Godwins were a noble dynasty firmly based in England: they were Sussex men. And although their rise to power started while England was part of a Scandinavian empire and they adapted well to the changed circumstances, the ambitions of most of them were confined to the English kingdom. The fate of the only one who seems to have imagined that he was a Dane, Godwin and Gytha's eldest son, Swegen, shows how wise the others were. And even their third son, Tostig, who married into the ruling family of Flanders and in 1066 allied with the king of Norway, was by then clearly an outsider. At the same time the sons of Godwin seem to have had a poor reputation in Scandinavia. For example, in the *Annales Estromenses* it is remarked that Duke Godwin sired from the sister of Duke Ulf 'the parricides Swegen, Tostig and Harold'.[1] Nevertheless, their Englishness should not be over emphasized. Godwin's children were Anglo–Danish by birth, and Harold's first consort came from East Anglia and may have been at least partly Scandinavian. They also travelled easily in the wider world. Godwin went to Denmark with the king; when exiled, he and his family found refuges in Ireland and Flanders. Harold and Tostig travelled far on the Continent; and after the conquest the survivors made new homes abroad. They were cosmopolitan English men and women. It would seem, however, that even well before 1066 England, under Edward, was slipping out of the Scandinavian world. The king and queen clearly had no northern interests. Only the sons of Ulf and Estrith, Earl Beorn and Osbeorn, seem to have remained in a quiet way attached to Denmark; and they were gone by 1049. Siward earl of Northumbria appears to have looked no farther than Scotland.

The year 1066 has always been regarded as the end of one era and the beginning of another. It was indeed for England a momentous twelve months. Not only did the royal line from Cerdic come to an end after some five-and-a-half centuries, to be replaced first by an English nobleman, Harold Earl of Wessex (just as the Carolingians had been replaced in Francia in 987 by Hugh Capet, duke of the Franks),[2] but also the new possessor of the throne was then quickly destroyed by a distant kinsman of the late King Edward, William duke of Normandy. Moreover, some of the detail of that eventful year is surprising. It was unusual for one king, let alone two, to be killed in battle and for one brother to kill another. The forebodings which the appearance of Halley's comet had aroused were amply confirmed.

There has, however, been some overstatement. The Anglo–Danish Harold has been called the last English king.[3] But the Norman William was not only king of England but also an English king — like the long line of his successors, whatever their racial make-up or origins may have been. And the events of 1066 also occurred within a lengthy period of instability for the English monarchy. Cnut was succeeded merely by two short-lived sons in turn. William the Conqueror fared similarly, although his second son, Henry I, ruled for 35 years. And the dynasty of the first Angevin king, Henry II, almost met the same fate when his second son, John, was destroyed by the invader, Louis VIII of France, who then came close to displacing John's child-heir, Henry III.

None of this, however, reduces the importance of the 'Norman' conquest of England. It was the prelude to great changes in the cultural, social and economic life of the kingdom and its orientation within Christendom. England was turned to face south-east rather than north. And the gradual conflation of the Germanic and Latin strains produced a richness and diversity in language and most other aspects of civilization that has since been the glory of England. The 'ifs' of history are not all that profitable.[4] But the sudden eclipse of the Godwins after the loss of a single battle in 1066 does invite speculation. If Duke William had been able to invade England in the summer, as clearly he had planned to do, he would have found Harold fresh and waiting to repel him with a fleet based on the Isle of Wight and an army on the Downs. And if Harold had then defeated William there would have been no Norman conquest with all its far-reaching consequences. Even if William had won, he would then have had to face Harold Hardrada and Tostig at the other end of the kingdom with unpredictable results. In this triangular contest the odds were on the survival of the Anglo–Danish polity, for even if Hardrada had come out on top, the linking of England with Norway would simply have intensified trends already set in motion by the Scandinavian settlements of the tenth century and the inclusion of England in Cnut's Danish empire.

Such possibilities were, however, extinguished by 'an arrow in the eye'. Although the rise of the Godwins from 'churl', to earl, to king in three generations, and then its sudden fall, could have been viewed as a cautionary tale of *hubris* and its punishment by the gods, it was naturally not so regarded by the family's encomiast, the author of *Vita*. For him the fatal flaw was not overweening ambition but disunity in the family, particularly the quarrel between Harold and Tostig. They just threw it all away. He started writing his tract for the queen one autumn, possibly in 1065, possibly in 1066, but probably not much later. Edward still seems to be alive at the beginning; but by the end not only he but also most of the other leading male actors are dead. The author, however, sees no farther into the future than a year and a day after the king's death when, as the dying king had prophesied, 'devils shall come through all this land with fire and sword and the havoc of war'.[5] The one consolation the author offers the queen is that her husband has gone straight to Heaven and is working miracles at his tomb. Edith, indeed, came through bereavement and the conquest comparatively well, surviving on her dower lands for nine years in honourable and comfortable retirement. Yet it cannot be thought that she regarded signs of her late husband's sanctity as adequate compensation for the future she had planned when she commissioned the writing of *Vita*.[6] And it may be, although the author is too discreet to inform us directly, that she blamed Harold for the sad ending. He had been too greedy and had paid insufficient attention to the interests of his kin.

Differing views have been, and can be, held of the Godwins. At one extreme, they culpably destroyed the Anglo–Saxon monarchy; at the other, they for long shored up the tottering kingship and perished in its defence. That they were ambitious cannot be doubted. And the simplest route to greatness was for Godwin to marry his daughter, Edith, to King Edward the Confessor. A son of this marriage would not only have re-endowed the monarchy with some of the Godwins' estates but would also have discouraged, if not completely extinguished, rival claims to the throne. When this simple plan failed, the family's ambitions were left in disarray, from which, it seems, they never recovered. It cannot be ascertained from *Vita* how the Godwins viewed the situation. The schism in the family in 1065 is not attributed to the problem of the succession to the throne. And no reference, overt or covert, to it seems to be made anywhere in the tract.

There was, indeed, no easy answer to the question who should succeed Edward at his death. It is clear that William of Normandy, Edward's cousin-once-removed through his mother

Emma, the daughter of Duke Richard I, had had his eye on the throne for some time; but he was almost without supporters in the kingdom. If Harold made a deal with him in 1064–5, it was not freely done and was repudiated once the earl was allowed home. King Swegen Estrithson of Denmark seems at times to have had hopes; but it would appear unlikely, even if Harold and his kin had wholeheartedly backed their cousin, that he could have succeeded, since Scandinavian invasions between 1066 and 1075 received little support from any section of the population. Another of Edward's great-nephews, Edgar Atheling, who had been recovered from Hungary in 1057 and educated probably in the royal court, can be considered the most 'natural' heir, and may indeed have been tacitly accepted by the Godwins as the heir presumptive. He was even elected king by a group in London after the battle of Hastings. Edgar was young and has been described as ineffectual and unsuitable, although the evidence for this is not strong. He was to have an adventurous career and prove himself an adroit survivor. He is unlikely to have been a worse king than Edward the Confessor, whom in some ways he resembles. Certainly if in 1066 Harold had put himself enthusiastically behind the atheling and set him up as a puppet king, as Godwin had with Edward, English history might have been very different. But it would not have prevented William's invasion nor necessarily an English defeat. In any case, in 1066, at a time of great danger, an apparently unanimous *witan* offered the crown to the experienced governor and soldier, Harold; and he accepted the challenge. He was in the flood-tide of his career. And he can hardly be blamed. It is, however, no surprise that Geoffrey of Cambrai, prior of Winchester Cathedral, who wrote tributes to Kings Cnut, Edward and William and their spouses, excluded Harold from his *Historical Epigrams*. Of the Godwins he commemorated only Queen Edith and her youngest brother, Wulfnoth.

Notes

1. *Annales Rerum Danicarum Estromenses* in *Scriptores Rerum Danicarum Medii Ævi*, ed. J. Langebek, i (Copenhagen, 1772), p. 236.
2. Harold is described on *BT*, pl. ii, as *dux Anglorum*, which may echo Hugh's title.
3. Julian Rathbone (1997) *The Last English King*. London: Abacus.
4. H.R. Loyn, *Harold, son of Godwin*, p. 13, produced a few. (Commemorative Lecture, Hastings and Bexhill Branch of the Historical Association, 1966.)
5. *Vita*, pp. 116–17.
6. Stafford, pp. 51, 260, however, regards Edith as anxious to portray her husband as a saint.

BIBLIOGRAPHY

Allen Brown, R. (ed.) (1979–89) *Proceedings of the Battle Conference on Anglo-Norman Studies, vols 1–11*. Woodbridge: Boydell.

Anscombe, A. (1913) The pedigree of Earl Godwin. *Transactions of the Royal Historical Society*, 3rd series, vii, 129–50.

Arnold, T. (ed.) (1882) *Symeon of Durham*, Historia Ecclesiae Dunelmensis. Rolls series. London: Master of the Rolls.

Ashdown, M. (1959) An Icelandic account of the survival of Harold Godwinson. In: P. Clemoes (ed.) *The Anglo-Saxons*. London: Bowes & Bowes, 122–36.

Barlow, F. (1979) *The English Church 1000–1066*. London: Longman.

Barlow, F. (1979) *The English Church 1066–1154*. London: Longman.

Barlow, F. (1983) Two notes: Cnut's second pilgrimage and Queen Emma's disgrace in 1043. *The Norman Conquest and Beyond*. London: Hambledon.

Barlow, F. (1997) *Edward the Confessor*. Yale English Monarchs series. London: Yale University Press.

Barlow, F. (1999) *The Feudal Kingdom of England 1042–1216*, 5th edn. London: Longman.

Barlow, F. (2000) *William Rufus*. Yale English Monarchs series. London: Yale University Press.

Barlow, F. (ed. and trans) (1992) *The Life of King Edward who Rests at Westminster*, 2nd edn. Oxford: Oxford Medieval Texts. [*Vita*]

Barlow, F. (ed. and trans) (1997) *The* Carmen de Hastingae Proelio *of Guy bishop of Amiens*. Oxford: Oxford Medieval Texts.

Barlow, L.W. (1957) The antecedents of Earl Godwine of Wessex. *New England Historical and Genealogical Register*, lxi, 32.

Baxter, S. (2001) The earls of Mercia and their commended men in the mid-eleventh century, *ANS*, xxiii, 23–40.

Beare, R. (1998) Earl Godwin's son as a barnacle goose. *Notes and Queries*, ccxlii, 459–62.

Beare, R. (1998) Swallows and barnacle geese. *Notes and Queries*, ccxliii, 5.

Beare, R. (1999) Which of Godwin's sons was called a barnacle goose? *Notes and Queries*, ccxliv, 5–6.

Beare, R. (2000) Godwin's sons as birds. *Prudentia*, xxxii, 1, 25–52.

Bell, A. (ed.) (1960) *Lestoire des Engleis par Geffrei Gaimar*, 3 vols. Oxford: Anglo-Norman Texts Society, xiv–xvi.

Bernstein, D. (1983) The blinding of Harold and the meaning of the Bayeux Tapestry. *Proceedings of the Battle Conference on Anglo-Norman Studies*, v, 40–64. Woodbridge: Boydell.

Blair, P.H. (1959) *An Introduction to Anglo-Saxon England*. Cambridge: Cambridge University Press.

Bloch, Marc (1923) La Vie de S. Edouard le Confesseur par Osbert de Clare. *Analecta Bollandiana*, xli, 114.

Brooke, G.C. (1932) *English Coins, from the Seventh Century to the Present Day*. London: Methuen.

Brown, V. (1994) *Rye Priory Cartulary and Charters*, 2 vols. Suffolk Records Society.

Bulwer Lytton, E. (1848) *Harold: the Last of the Saxon Kings*. London: Routledge.

Campbell, A. (ed.) (1949) *Encomium Emmae Reginae*. Royal Historical Society Camden 3rd ser., lxxii. London: Royal Historical Society.

Chibnall, M. (ed.) (1969–80) *Orderic Vitalis*: Historia Ecclesiastica, 6 vols. Oxford: Oxford Medieval Texts.

Chibnall, M. (ed.) (1990–95) *Proceedings of the Battle Conference on Anglo-Norman Studies, vols 12–16*. Woodbridge: Boydell.

Clarke, P.A. (1994) *The English Nobility under Edward the Confessor*. Oxford: Clarendon.

Clay, C.T. (1942) *Early Yorkshire Charters, iv*, The House of Richmond. Leeds: Yorkshire Archaeological Society.

Clemoes, P. (ed.) (1959) *The Anglo-Saxons. Studies in Some Aspects of Their History and Culture*. London: Bowes & Bowes.

Darlington, R.R. (ed.) (1928) *The* Vita Wulfstani *of William of Malmesbury*. Royal Historical Society, Camden 3rd ser., xl. London: Royal Historical Society.

Darlington, R.R. and McGurk, P. (eds) (1995) *The Chronicle of John of Worcester*, trans. J. Bray and P. McGurk. Oxford: Oxford Medieval Texts.

Davies, R.H. (1967) The lands and rights of Harold son of Godwine, and their distribution by William I. A study in the Domesday evidence. (Unpublished M.A. Dissertation, University College, Cardiff.)

Davis, H.W.C. and Whitwell, R.J. (1913) *Regesta Regum Anglorum 1066–1154.* Oxford: Clarendon Press.

Davis, R.H.C. and Chibnall, M. (eds and trans) (1998) *The Gesta Guillelmi of William of Poitiers.* Oxford: Oxford Medieval Texts.

de Gray Birch, W. (1882) *Liber Vitae: Register and Martyrology of New Minster and Hyde Abbey, Winchester.* Hampshire Record Society, p. 22.

de Gray Birch, W. (ed.) (1885) *Vita Haroldi. Three Lives of the Last Englishmen,* trans. M. Swanton 1984.

Delisle, L. (ed.) (1909) Rouleau mortuaire du B. Vital, abbé de Savigny. Paris, pl. xxxviii, tit. 153.

Dickinson, F.H. (1876) The sale of Combe. *Proceedings of the Somerset Archaeological and Natural History Society,* xxii, 106–13.

Dimock, J.F. (1868) *Giraldus Cambrensis,* Descriptio Kambriae, in *Omnia Opera.* Rolls series, vi, 217. London: Master of the Rolls.

Dodwell, R. (1965) Article in *The Observer* Supplement, 31 October 1965, pp. 21–2.

Douglas, D.C. (1964) *William the Conqueror.* London: Eyre & Spottiswoode.

Douglas, D.C. (ed.) (1979) *English Historical Documents.* London: Eyre Methuen, vol. i, *c.* 500–1042, ed. D. Whitelock, vol. ii, 1042–1189, ed. Douglas and G.W. Greenaway (2nd edn, 1981).

Duffy, S. (1998) Ireland's Hastings: the Anglo-Norman Conquest of Dublin. *Proceedings of the Battle Conference on Anglo-Norman Studies,* xx.

Edwards, E. (ed.) (1866) *Chronica monasterii de Hida* in *Liber monasterii de Hyda.* Rolls series, 283–321. London: Master of the Rolls.

Ellis, H. (ed.) (1859) *Chronica Johannis de Oxenedes, with the history of the Abbey of St Benet Holme to 1275*. Rolls series, p. 293. London: Master of the Rolls.

Fisher, D.J.V. (1973) *The Anglo-Saxon Age*. London: Longman.

Fleming, R. (1983) Domesday estates of the king and the Godwinesons: a study in late Saxon politics. *Speculum*, lviii, 254–76.

Fleming, R. (1991) *Kings and Lords in Conquest England*. Cambridge: Cambridge University Press.

Fleming, R. (2001) The new wealth, the new rich and the new political style in late Anglo-Saxon England, *ANS*, xxiii, 1–22.

Foreville, R. (1952) Aux origines de la renaissance juridique et influences romanisantes chez Guillaume de Poitiers, biographe du Conquérant. *Moyen Age*, lviii, 43–83.

Foreville, R. (1979) Le sacre des rois anglo-normands et angevins et le serment du sacre, XIe–XIIe siècles. *Proceedings of the Battle Conference on Anglo-Norman Studies*, i, 49–62. Woodbridge: Boydell.

Fowke, F.R. (1898) *The Bayeux Tapestry: a History and Description*. In White Ex-Libris series, 80.

Freeman, E.A. (1877) *History of the Norman Conquest of England*, 3rd edn. Oxford: Clarendon Press.

Gardiner, M. (2000) Shipping and trade between England and the Continent during the eleventh century. *Proceedings of the Battle Conference on Anglo-Norman Studies*, xxii, 77. Woodbridge: Boydell.

Garmonsway, G.N. (1953, 1972) *The Anglo-Saxon Chronicle*. London: Everyman Press.

Grierson, P. (1936) A visit of Earl Harold to Flanders in 1056. *English Historical Review*, li, 90–7.

Gubbin, G.P., Conner, P.W. *et al.* (1996) *The Anglo-Saxon Chronicle: a collaborative edition in 23 vols*. Cambridge: Cambridge University Press.

Hamilton, N.E.S.A. (ed.) (1870) William of Malmesbury, *De Gestis Pontificum Anglorum*. Rolls ser. London: Master of the Rolls.

Harper-Bill, C. (1996–2000) *Proceedings of the Battle Conference on Anglo-Norman Studies, vols 17–22*. Woodbridge: Boydell.

Hart, C. (2000) The Bayeux Tapestry and schools of illumination at Canterbury. *Proceedings of the Battle Conference on Anglo-Norman Studies*, xxii, 117–68. Woodbridge: Boydell.

Hart, C.R. (1997) William Malet and his family. *Proceedings of the Battle Conference on Anglo-Norman Studies*, xix, 123–65. Woodbridge: Boydell.

Haskins, C.H. (1922) King Harold's books. *English Historical Review*, xxxvii, 398–400.

Haskins, C.H. (1927) *Studies in the History of Medieval Science*, 2nd edn (Harvard Historical Studies, vol. 27). Cambridge, MA: Harvard University.

Hearne, T. (1723) *Hemingi Chartularium Ecclesiae Wigorniensis*. Oxford.

Hindle, H. (1868) *Historia translationis S. Cuthberti*, cap. 5. Surtees Society, li.

Hudson, B. (1979) The family of Harold Godwineson: a study in late Saxon politics. *Royal Society of Antiquaries of Ireland*, cix, 92–100.

James, M.R. (trans.) (1923) *De Nugis Curialium. Hon. Soc. of Cymmrodorion*, rec. series, ix.

Keats-Rohan, K.S.B. (1991) William I and the Breton contingent in the non-Norman Conquest, 1060–1087. *Proceedings of the Battle Conference on Anglo-Norman Studies*, xiii, 164. Woodbridge: Boydell.

Kemble, J.M. (1849) *The Saxons in England*, 2 vols. London.

Kemble, J.M. (ed.) (1839–48) *Codex Diplomaticus Aevi Saxonici*, 6 vols. London: English Historical Society.

Keynes, S. (1980) *The Diplomas of King Æthelred 'the Unready', 978–1016*. Cambridge: Cambridge University Press.

Keynes, S. (1998) Regenbald the Chancellor (*sic*). *Proceeding of the Battle Conference on Anglo-Norman Studies*, x, 201–3. Woodbridge: Boydell.

Knowles, D., Brooke, C.N.L. and London, V.C.M. (eds) (1972) *The Heads of Religious Houses, England and Wales, 940–1216*. Cambridge: Cambridge University Press.

Körner, S. (1964) *The Battle of Hastings: England and Europe 1035–1066*. Lund: Gleerup.

Laing, S. (ed.) (1964) *Heimskringla*. Revised. London: Dent. New York: Dutton.

Langebek, J. (ed.) (1772) *Annales Rerum Danicarum Estromenses* in *Scriptores Rerum Danicarum Medii Aevi*. Copenhagen, p. 236.

Lappenberg, J.M. (1876) *Gesta Hammaburgensis Ecclesiae of Adam of Bremen*, 2nd edn. Hanover.

Lappenberg, J.M. (trans. B. Thorpe) (1845) *A History of England under the Anglo-Saxon Kings*, 2 vols. London: John Murray.

Larson, L.M. (1912) *Canute the Great*. In: Abbott, E. *Heroes of the Nations*. New York: Putnam.

Lawn, B. (1979) *The Prose Salernitan Questions* (Bodleian Library MS Auct.F.3.10). London: Oxford University Press/British Academy.

Lawson, M.K. (1993) *Cnut, The Danes in England in the early eleventh century*. The Medieval World series. Harlow: Longman.

Lloyd, J.E. (1899–1900) Wales and the coming of the Normans, 1039–93. *Transactions of the Hon. Soc. of Cymmrodorion*, 369–73.

Lloyd, J.E. (1939) *A History of Wales from the Earliest Times to the Edwardian Conquest*, 3rd edn. London: Longman.

Lot, F. (ed.) (1894) *Hariulf of Saint-Riquier*, Chronicon Cetulense. *Collection des Textes pour servir à l'étude et à l'enseignement de l'histoire*. Paris.

Love, R.C. (1996) Three Eleventh-century Anglo-Latin Saints' Lives. Oxford: Oxford University Press.

Loyn, H.R. (1962) *Anglo-Saxon England and the Norman Conquest*. London: Longman.

Loyn, H.R. (1966) *Harold son of Godwin*. Lecture, Hastings and Bexhill Branch, Historical Association. 1066 Commemoration Series No. 2.

Macray, W.D. (ed.) (1863) Translation and miracles of S. Odulph. *Chronicon Abbatiae de Evesham*, 317–18. Rolls series. London: Master of the Rolls.

Magnusson, M. and Pálsson, H. (ed. and trans) (1966) *Harald Sigurdsson, King Harald's Saga*. London: Penguin Classics.

Maund, K.L. (1989) The Welsh alliances of Earl Ælfgar of Mercia. *Proceedings of the Battle Conference on Anglo-Norman Studies*, xi, 183–4. Woodbridge: Boydell.

Migne, J.P. (ed.) (1844) *Patrologiae Cursus Completus, Patrologia Latina*, 221 vols, Paris.

Muntz, H. (1949) *The Golden Warrior: the Story of Harold and William.* London: Chatto & Windus.

Mynors, R.A.B., Thomson, R.M. and Winterbottom, M. (eds and trans) (1998) *William of Malmesbury* De Gestis Regum Anglorum. Oxford: Oxford Medieval Texts.

Nelson, J.L. (1982) The rites of the conqueror. *Proceedings of the Battle Conference on Anglo-Norman Studies*, iv, 123–9. Woodbridge: Boydell.

Nip, R. (1999) Political relations between England and Flanders. *Proceedings of the Battle Conference on Anglo-Norman Studies*, xxi, 150.

Offler, H.S. (1968) *Durham Episcopal Charters, 1071–1152.* Surtees Society, clxxix.

Olrik, J. and Raeder, H. (eds) (1931) *Gesta Danorum of Saxo Grammaticus.* Copenhagen.

Olsen, M. (1908) Runestenen ved Oddernes Kirke. *Afhandlinger viede Sophus Bugges Minde.* Christiania.

Palgrave, F. (1832) *A History of the Anglo-Saxons.* Reissued 1887. London: Ward, Lock.

Plummer, C. and Earle, J. (1892) *Two of the Saxon Chronicles Parallel.* 2 vols. Oxford: Clarendon Press.

Pollock, J. (1996) *Harold: Rex. Is King Harold II buried in Bosham Church?* Bosham: Penny Royal Publications.

Rathbone, J. (1997) *The Last English King.* London: Little, Brown.

Rees, W.J. (1853) *Vita Sancti Gundleii*, cap. 13 in *Lives of the Cambro-British Saints.* Welsh Manuscripts Society, 153–4.

Rogers, N. (1992) The Waltham Abbey Relic List. In: C. Hicks (ed.) *England in the Eleventh Century.* Stamford: Paul Watkins.

Ronay, G. (1989) *The Lost King of England.* Woodbridge: Boydell.

Round, J.H. (1895) *Feudal England. Historical Studies on the Eleventh and Twelfth Centuries.* London: Swan Sonnenschein.

Round, J.H. (1930) *Family Origins and Other Studies*, ed. W. Page. London: Constable.

Rule, M. (ed.) (1884) *Eadmeri Historia Novorum in Anglia.* Rolls series, pp. 6–8. London: Master of the Rolls.

Sawyer, P.H. (1968) *Anglo-Saxon Charters: an Annotated List and Bibliography.* London: Royal Historical Society.

Sawyer, P.H. (1970) *From Roman Britain to Norman England.* London: Methuen.

Schmitt, F.S. (ed.) (1946–52) *S. Anselmi Opera Omnia.* Edinburgh: Thomas Nelson.

Searle, E. (1981) Women and the legitimization of succession at the Norman Conquest. *Proceedings of the Battle Conference on Anglo-Norman Studies,* iii, 161–2. Woodbridge: Boydell.

Senecal, C. (2001) Keeping up with the Godwinesons: in pursuit of aristocratic status in late Anglo-Saxon England, *ANS,* xxiii, 251–66.

Sherley-Price, L. (trans) (1955, 1968) *Bede: A History of the English Church and People.* London: Penguin Classics.

Southern, R.W. (1953) *The Making of the Middle Ages.* London: Hutchinson.

Stafford, P. (1997) *Queen Emma and Queen Edith.* Oxford: Blackwell.

Stenton, F. (1922) St Benet of Holme and the Norman Conquest. *English Historical Review,* xxxvii, 225–35.

Stenton, F.M. *et al.* (1965) *The Bayeux Tapestry: a Comprehensive Survey,* 2nd edn. London: Phaidon.

Stenton, F.M. (1943, 1947, 1971) *Anglo-Saxon England.* Oxford: Oxford University Press.

Stevenson, J. (ed.) (1841) *Liber Vitae ecclesie Dunelmensis,* Surtees Soc., xiii.

Strickland, M. (1997) Military technology and conquest: the anomaly of Anglo-Saxon England. *Proceedings of the Battle Conference on Anglo-Norman Studies,* xix, 353–82. Woodbridge: Boydell.

Stubbs, W. (ed.) (1861) *The Foundation of Waltham Abbey. The Tract 'De Inventione Sanctae Crucis nostrae in Monte Acuto et de ductione eiusdem apud Waltham'.* Oxford.

Stubbs, W. (ed.) (1874) *Memorials of St Dunstan, archbishop of Canterbury.* Rolls series, 141–2. London: Master of the Rolls.

Stubbs, W. (ed.) (1887–9) William of Malmesbury, *De Gestis Regum Anglorum.* Rolls series. London: Master of the Rolls.

Swanton, M. (trans and introduced) (1984) *Three Lives of the Last Englishmen.* London: Garland.

Taylor, A.J. (1992) Belrem. *Proceedings of the Battle Conference on Anglo-Norman Studies*, xiv, 1–23. Woodbridge: Boydell.

Tennyson, A. (1877) *Harold, a Drama*.

Thorpe, B. (ed.) (1861) *Anglo-Saxon Chronicle*. Rolls series. London: Master of the Rolls.

Turner, S. (1820) *The History of the Anglo-Saxons*, 3 vols, 3rd edn.

van Houts, E.M.C. (ed.) (1997) *Brevis Relatio de Guillelmo nobilissimo comite Normannorum*. Camden Miscellany, xxxiv, Camden 5th ser., x, 1–48.

van Houts, E.M.C. (ed.) (1992–5) *The* Gesta Normannorum Ducum *of William of Jumièges, Orderic Vitalis, and Robert of Torigni*, 2 vols. Oxford: Oxford Medieval Texts.

van Houts, E.M.C. (1988) The ship list of William the Conqueror. *Proceedings of the Battle Conference on Anglo-Norman Studies*, x, 159–83. Woodbridge: Boydell.

Wade-Evans, A.W. (1944) *Vitae Sanctorum Britanniae et Genealogiae. Vita Sancti Gundleii*, 184–6.

Walcot, M.E.C. (1873) Inventory of Waltham Holy Cross. *Transactions of the Essex Archaeological Society*, 257–64.

Walker, I.W. (1997) *Harold, the last Anglo-Saxon King*. Stroud: Sutton.

Watkiss, L. and Chibnall, M. (ed. and trans) (1994) *The Waltham Chronicle*. Oxford: Clarendon Press.

Webb, C.C.J. (1932) *John of Salisbury*, Johannis Saresbiriensis episcopi Carnotensis Policraticus. Great Medieval Churchmen Series. London: Methuen.

Whitelock, D. (ed.) (1952) *Sermo Lupi ad Anglos*, 2nd edn. Methuen's Old English Library.

Whitelock, D. (ed.) *English Historical Documents*, vol. i, *c.* 500–1042. London: Eyre and Spottiswoode.

Whitelock, D., Douglas, D.C. and Tucker, S.I. (eds) (1961) *The Anglo-Saxon Chronicle*. London: Eyre and Spottiswoode.

Williams, A. (1995) *The English and the Norman Conquest*. Woodbridge: Boydell.

Williams, A. (1981) Land and power in the eleventh century: the estates of Harold Godwineson. *Proceedings of the Battle Conference on Anglo-Norman Studies*, iii, 162–3. Woodbridge: Boydell.

Williams, A. (1997) The spoliation of Worcester. *Proceedings of the Battle Conference on Anglo-Norman Studies*, xix, 385–6. Woodbridge: Boydell.

Wright, C.E. (1939) *The Cultivation of Saga in Anglo-Saxon England*. Edinburgh: Oliver & Boyd.

Wright, T. (1850) Water Mapes, *De Nugis Curialium*. London: The Camden Society, l.

Wright, T. (ed.) (1872) *The Anglo-Latin Satirical Poets and Epigrammatists of the Twelfth Century*. Rolls series. London: Master of the Rolls.

INDEX